A PERSON IS A PRODUCT OF TIME, PLACE, AND CIRCUMSTANCES

BOOKS BY ALLA P. GAKUBA, BSCE, MAS, PhD

Trilogy: motivational nonfiction short stories to teach logic, creativity, new skills, and self-esteem that would change readers lives:

What Is Life? What Is Happiness?
(Book 1)

A Person Is a Product of Time, Place, and Circumstances
(Book 2)

How to Design Innovations and Solve Business and Personal Problems
(Book 3)

A PERSON IS A PRODUCT OF TIME, PLACE, AND CIRCUMSTANCES

Book 2 in the trilogy: motivational nonfiction short stories to teach logic, creativity, new skills, and self-esteem that would change readers lives

Alla P. Gakuba, BSCE, MAS, PhD

Copyright © 2015 by Alla P. Gakuba, BSCE, MAS, PhD
All rights reserved.
Library of Congress Catalogue-in-Publication Data
Gakuba, Alla P., BSCE, MAS, PhD
A Person Is a product of Time, Place, and Circumstances. Book 2 in the trilogy: motivational nonfiction short stories to teach logic, creativity, new skills, and self-esteem that would change readers lives / Alla P. Gakuba, BSCE, MAS, PhD. First edition.

pages cm
Published by Knowhow Skills, San Francisco Bay, California, USA;
www.allapgakuba.com

Hardcover: ISBN 978-1-943131-15-0
Paperback: ISBN 978-1-943131-11-2
Kindle: ISBN 978-1-943131-12-9
PDF: ISBN 978-1-943131-13-6
EPUB: ISBN 978-1-943131-14-3

LCCN: 2015905239
1. Self-Help – Personal Growth – General. 2. Self-Help – Motivational. 3. Politics & Social Sciences – Politics & Government – International & World Politics – Russian & the Former Soviet Union. I. Title.
KEYWORDS: 1. Motivational stories. 2. Self-esteem. 3. American women. 4. Russian Revolution 1917. 5. Soviet Union & Russia.

First Edition 2015

Book designed by Marian Oprea

Printed in the United States of America

10 9 8 7 6 5 4 3 2 1

To my grandsons Paris and Apollo,

with expectations that they will grow into fine men of dignity and honor who will not live selfish lives, but instead will have a purpose in life and make contributions to society, the country, and the world.

TABLE OF CONTENTS

ABOUT AUTHOR 1

PREFACE 5

A GUIDE TO READING THIS BOOK 9

SHORT STORY #1
A Person Is a Product of Time, Place, and Circumstances 13

SHORT STORY #2
Everything Happens for the Best.
Or, Embrace Events and Challenges 24

SHORT STORY #3
Self-Esteem and Maslow's Theory.
Or, an Elephant and a Poodle 43

SHORT STORY #4
Risk: to Take or Not to Take? Or, Once You Take a Risk,
Your Probability of Success Goes from 0% to 50% 54

SHORT STORY #5
Everything Has a Limit.
Or, How Much Stress Can Our Brain and Body Take? 67

SHORT STORY #6
The Civil Rights Act of 1964 and the
Equal Employment Opportunity Commission 82

SHORT STORY #7
How American Women Overtook American Men
in Just 2 Generations 92

SHORT STORY #8
The Great Event of the 20th Century that Changed
the World: Vladimir Ilyich Lenin and
the Russian Revolution of November 6–7, 1917 104

Table of Contents

SHORT STORY #9
Technological Invention That Shocked the
World in the 20th Century. Or, the Russians
Launched Sputnik on October 4, 1957_____ 126

SHORT STORY #10
Why Was the Soviet Union Fighting in Afghanistan
Before the USA?_____ 133

SHORT STORY #11
The Greatest Catastrophe of the 20th Century.
Or, How the Soviet Union Disintegrated in 1991_____ 142

SHORT STORY #12
It Is Easy to Despair, but the Best Traits of
the Human Character Are Not to Give Up.
But Instead to Stand Up, Fight Back, and Save Yourself_____ 182

SHORT STORY #13
A Fly in a Bottle. Or, If Only I Knew it Before_____ 196

SHORT STORY #14
Return of the Sound. Or, Shocking News _____ 201

SHORT STORY #15
Ability Is Nothing Without Opportunity _____ 207

SHORT STORY #16
Why Is Engineering the Most Prestigious Profession
in the World, Except in the USA?_____ 220

SHORT STORY #17
What Is National Wealth? How National Wealth Created?
Who Creates National Wealth?_____ 236

SHORT STORY #18
How Many Millionaires Are in the USA? What Types?_____ 249

SHORT STORY #19
What Is Amok? Or, Housing Amok_____ 263

SHORT STORY #20
Why Do Immigrants in the USA Speak with Foreign Accents? _____ 271

    ACKNOWLEDGEMENTS _____ 277

    ILLUSTRATION CREDITS _____ 279

    THE AUTHOR'S, ALLA P. GAKUBA, BSCE, MAS, PhD,
    CONTRIBUTIONS TO ENGINEERING,
    TO NATIONAL WEALTH, AND TO WOMEN:
    The Forces of Innovation…Conflict? _____ 283

    HAVE YOU READ? BOOKS BY
    ALLA P. GAKUBA, BSCE, MAS, PhD _____ 289

ABOUT AUTHOR

△ △ △

When attending civil engineering university in her native city Odessa, on the Black Sea, the Soviet Union, the author, Alla P. Gakuba lived an ordinary life. She was a shy, timid, and unsure of herself young woman, but a serious student.

Fascinated with life, bubbled with infinite youth energy, and curious about the world, she had read hundreds classic books written by world famous classical writers.

She saw numerous movies, the majority of them international, and went to the theater many times to hear the most popular operas, saw ballet performances, not to mention visits to the drama theatre, the circuses, and philharmonic classical music performances, all from a young age.

She was a dreamer...In her dreams she was anything she wanted to be. Intoxicated by life she imitated her heroes and adopted their manner, language, attitudes, and became as sophisticated as they were.

Then, one cold, unassuming November evening, fate suddenly interfered and changed her destiny. Fate propelled her to live on different continents, ambushed

About Author

her with life-threatening events and monumental problems.[1] She survived, became stoic, and make many contributions.

Alla worked in 4 countries: the Soviet Union, Rwanda, Tanzania, and the United States; in 3 languages: Russian, French, and English; and under 2 radical systems: socialism and capitalism.

Alla P. Gakuba, received her BSCE from Odessa Civil Engineering University in the Soviet Union; she earned her master's degree at Johns Hopkins University, Baltimore; and she received her PhD from George Washington University, Washington, D.C.

Some of Alla P. Gakuba's, BSCE, MAS, PhD, contributions to: engineering, healthcare, and women:

- △ She designed alone, one person, a 10-span bridge with 4 ramps, I-95, in downtown Baltimore, over the Patapsco River.
- △ She found the solution how to design "a spiral" and then designed it for 3.5 miles of the Baltimore subway aerial structure which is considered to be the most challenging engineering design.
- △ She was the 1st woman to receive a PhD in the Management of Science, Technology, and Innovations field.

About Author

- △ Her dissertation is considered to be in the top 5% among 250–300 dissertations written in the last 15 years.
- △ In health care, Alla P. Gakuba created several innovations. One of her innovations sparked an entirely new industry. It created hundreds of thousands of new jobs. As it grew, it started bringing millions, and then billions, of dollars yearly in new revenue to many companies.
- △ Please see more author's contributions at the end of this book. Alla P. Gakuba's contributions to engineering, to national wealth, and to women: *The Forces of Innovation...Conflict?* by Carissa Giblin, article provided by the Society of Women Engineers, *The Florida Engineering Journal, January 2004.*

---

[1] About Alla P. Gakuba's life-threatening events and monumental problems please read her short story # 7: "What Is Happiness? Or, What Were the Happiest Years of Your Life?" in Book 1 (the trilogy): *What is Life? What is Happiness?*

PREFACE

△ △ △

I wrote this book with one intention—to enlarge my readers' knowledge and raise their sophistication to a higher level. After reading this book, they will be able to solve difficult problems and challenge life's stressful events—so for them life will be much easier than it was for me.

A Person Is a Product of Time, Place, and Circumstances is a title of this book, as is the name of one of *the Laws of Life* stories in this book. This law is very much applicable to American women and personally to me.

In 1964 the Civil Rights Act was created that, for the 1st time in American history, gave an equal opportunity to women and minorities. To enforce the Civil Rights Act, the Equal Employment Opportunity Commission, EEOC, was established in 1965.

Millions of women took this opportunity and risk and entered labor force and colleges to compete in hostile men domineering environments. Time: the historic 1964–1990s. Place: the USA. Circumstances: Civil Rights Act of 1964 gave women equal opportunity with men. Women were put to a test: to fail or to succeed.

Women stoicism, perseverance, endurance, and focus paid of. Amazingly, they succeeded—in less than 2 generations! Today 60% American women are graduating with college degrees versus 40% of American men.

And who are on the deans lists of best students? Women are, majority on the lists are women. Today more women are employed than men, and women are more financially savvy than men, especially younger women.

I was also a product of time, place, and circumstances. My professional contributions cannot be attributed to myself only. I was a product of this *Law of Life*. The time was: 1970s–1990s. The place: the USA where the Civil Rights Act of 1964 was created, and equal opportunity was taking hold. I was working as a structural engineer in an all-male profession. Circumstances: I was a Russian in the USA during the Cold War, where a great technological and political competition were taking place between 2 superpowers, the USA and the Soviet Union, for dominance of the world

Every company wanted to hire me to see the difference between American and Russian engineers. I was given an opportunity, and I lived up to their expectations. "Ability is nothing without opportunity" is another educational story in this book.

There are more short stories based on my know-how skills and experience: when to take or not to take a risk; what is self-esteem and Maslow's theory; what is the great 20th-century event that changed the world; what is national wealth; what is engineering; what is the greatest

Preface

catastrophe of the 20th century; how not to get despair, but instead stand up, fight back, and save yourself; why do immigrants in the USA speak with foreign accents; and many more educational stories.

After I finished writing this book, I had a problem: Could my readers easily interpret the title of my book? To find the answer I tested it on one of my new acquaintances in a club, Sam.

To catch him off guard, I put this book title to the test. "Sam," I asked, "do you understand what my book title *A Person Is a Product of Time, Place, and Circumstances* means?" I knew that he needed some time to think and process my question.

Impatient, I started giving him some clues. "Look, imagine if you were born at the beginning of the 20th century and not at the end? You would be a different person. You could be a farmer, performing manual labor with an average life expectancy of 45 years.

"Still, you would be lucky being a man. If you were a woman at that time, you would be a farmer's wife and die before your husband from bearing and rearing many children, as well as enduring much of the heavy farm work. At that time many farmers outlived 2, 3, or 4 of their wives."

"Oh, yes, I know," Sam interrupted me. "Even if I were born today as a black man, my life would be completely different. I would not have many opportunities." With this statement, Sam solved my problem.

This book is especially important to younger generations who are wasting their time and lives on the fluff of social media, texting, and *Hannah Montana*—which do not lend themselves to acquiring and retaining real knowledge.

After reading this book readers will become well-informed and sophisticated, will be able to solve difficult problems, will contest life-challenging events, and will start believing in themselves. Listen to one whose wisdom and experience offers *The Laws of Life*.

Alla P. Gakuba, BSCE, MAS, PhD
San Francisco Bay, California, USA

A GUIDE TO READING THIS BOOK

△ △ △

This is a book 2 in the trilogy[1] of motivational nonfiction short stories to teach logic, creativity, new skills, and self-esteem that would change readers lives.

It consists of 20 different nonfiction know-how short stories.

Readers have 2 options when reading those stories. The 1st option is to read them in sequential order, that is, one story after another. The 2nd option is to scan the Table of Contents and choose which story to read 1st.

Readers will notice short, repetitive facts in some of the stories. That was done intentionally to ease the flow of reading, instead of referring readers to different stories for facts.

At the end of each story, there is a summary—*The moral of the story*—which states what this particular story is teaches and what questions it answers.

---

[1] Book 1 in the trilogy: *What Is a Life? What Is Happiness?*
Book 3 in the trilogy: *How to Design Innovations to Solve Business and Personal Problems.*

A PERSON IS A PRODUCT OF TIME, PLACE, AND CIRCUMSTANCES

SHORT STORY

A Person Is a Product of Time, Place, and Circumstances

△ △ △

When I was a teenager, I read memoirs of Napoleon Bonaparte and was fascinated with his ideas; it was imprinted in my mind for many years. Napoleon Bonaparte (1769–1821) is considered one of the world's greatest military leaders, a military genius, and the First Emperor of France. His objective was to conquer the world and unite the fragmented and fighting countries of Europe under one nation, the French Empire.

In his memoirs, he attributed all his conquests and achievements not to his genius, or special military gifts he was born with, but, instead to time, place, and circumstances.

How Did Napoleon Bonaparte Become "A Product of Time, Place, and Circumstances?"

What were the time, place, and circumstances responsible for Napoleon Bonaparte (1769–1821), a Corsican, to rise to the military rank of a general in the French Army, greatly expand the French Empire, and become the First Emperor of France?

The time was the French Revolution, a turbulent and uncertain period. The place was France. Circumstances: there were many circumstances responsible for Napoleon's rise and fall.

A Person Is a Product of Time, Place, and Circumstances

Napoleon was born in Corsica; his father was a lawyer and sent him to French college in Autun, then to a Military Academy in France.[1] Napoleon lived in France during a dynamic, tumultuous, and historic time. French King Louis was financing the American Revolution (1775–1783), and was fighting his great enemy—the British—on American, not on French, soil.

The King bankrupted France and heavily taxed his subjects. Impoverished and frustrated mobs stormed the Bastille, freed all its political prisoners and the French Revolution began in 1789.

In 1793, France became a Republic whose one of the mottos was: Liberte, Egalite, Fraternite (Freedom, Equality, and Brotherhood). The motto ignited a historical interpretation of the French Revolution, and the opposition and rivalry between Liberals and Socialists began. The King was executed, and Queen Marie Antoinette was sent to the guillotine.

Napoleon, after the French Revolution, was on Italy's side, fighting with the Corsican resistance against French occupation. When disappointed with the Corsican civil war, he returned to France in 1793, and joined the French Army. To enhance his French national profile, in 1796 he married Josephine de Beauharnais, (1763–1814), a French socialite and the widow of a French general.

He supported a far-left, popular movement, and his military career bloomed. He vanquished royalists who were fighting inside France to revert the French Republic back to a monarchy. Napoleon occupied Egypt, and then greatly expanded the French Empire to Italy, Holland, Sweden, and Spain and became a great military star.

In 1800, the new French constitution was implemented with the Napoleonic Code, which allowed for freedom of religion and equal opportunity for government jobs based not on birth privileges, but on merit and skills. He reformed France's economy, as well as its legal and educational systems. His popularity grew after he instituted the Napoleonic Code, and in 1802 he became the First French Emperor.

Napoleon's objective was to conquer Europe, and he succeeded. He took all Europe and then marched on Russia, but was defeated by the Russians in 1812. After defeat, he lost his empire and was exiled to the island of Elba. He escaped and regained his power, but at Waterloo he was handed his final defeat by the British and Prussians.

He was sent into exile for the 2nd time, this time to the small windy and dusty island of St. Helena located 2,000 kilometers from West Africa, in the South Atlantic Ocean, ruled by the British. On St. Helena he wrote his memoirs and created a legend around himself.

Indeed, Napoleon was a product of time, place, and circumstances. He was lucky: he was born to a wealthy family that paid for his education; he lived during the changing and uncertain time of the French Revolution's turmoil, where quick changes and achievements were made, and so quickly were disbanded and lost. Such a dynamic environment created many new circumstances available for individuals to take advantage of. The French monarchy was overthrown, resulting in an open field for opportunists. Napoleon took this opportunity.

There was 1 significant drawback for Napoleon however—he was a Corsican, not a Frenchman. Fighting in the French Army set him up for fearless military battles to defeat French oppositions and conquer new territories for France, so no Frenchmen could question his national origin or loyalty. He achieved his personal goals and became a military general and the First Emperor of France.

Later, fate changed his destiny; he was defeated and lost his French Empire, and died in exile on the island of St. Helena. On the island, he wrote his memoirs where he accredited his achievements to time, place, and circumstances.

American Women and Time, Place, and Circumstances

How did American women become "a product of time, place, and circumstances?" starting from 1964? In 1918, women were given the right to vote for the 1st time in American history. But there were no decrees for jobs and education.

The Civil Rights Act of 1964 against job discrimination in hiring and firing regardless of sex or gender was signed into law by Democratic President Lyndon Johnson. Then, to implement this law, in 1965 the Equal Employment Opportunity Commission, EEOC, was created. These laws covered both groups, women and minorities.

The Civil Rights Act of 1964 was on the books, but for many years the law met great resistance and was difficult to implement. It was only in 1968 when the 1st American woman was accepted to Yale, or 4 years after the passage of the Civil Rights Act.

Women took matters into their own hands; they organized and started hundreds of different women's associations and support groups to learn, obtain new skills, and become informed about the world around them.

The brightest started entering colleges. Soon their ranks swelled and 2 generations later, they made spectacular progress with 60% of women graduating with college degrees versus 40% of American men.

Just watch the *Court TV* shows and hear and see judges comment that in their practice, they see very few men as plaintiffs. Plaintiffs are always women; they loaned money to boyfriends, men friends, or men relatives.

Women are watching their financial guru, Suze Orman, and are buying all her books. Very few men have heard, or know about Suze Orman.

A Person Is a Product of Time, Place, and Circumstances

Implementing the Civil Rights Act of 1964 was difficult. Women fought for their rights and place in companies for many years. Today, young women have no idea of the everyday discrimination in the workplace women faced in the beginning.

I also was a product of time, place, and circumstances at the beginning of my career. Time and place: it was the beginning of the 1970s when I arrived in the USA. Even the Civil Rights Act of 1964 was created, but was very difficult to implement.

The working environment was hostile, especially for women engineers. There were no women structural engineers in companies at that time. These brilliant pioneers who had received engineering degrees were not hired.

My circumstances: I was lucky—I was a Russian. There was an ongoing Cold War and fierce competitions for technological progress and dominance of the world between 2 adversaries: the USA and the Soviet Union.

Who will win? Capitalism or socialism? Soviet engineering and science was the best in the world and American engineers paid closed attention to it. I was hired for one reason: a top management wanted to see the difference between American and Russian engineers.

At the same time, my peers—the male engineers—did not like this top management's decision. They angrily objected. All day they gathered in groups near my station, loudly expressing their scorn towards me; they thought that now their profession was going downhill because a woman was going to design a bridge.

I could not take such pressure, nor could I concentrate in such a hostile work environment, and after 3–4 days almost left. The human resources manager, who hired me, intervened and brought this problem to the top management.

For the next several days, they called men in groups to a meeting room explaining the Civil Rights Act law of 1964, and warning them about the consequences. If they failed to comply they would be fired for continuing their actions. Slowly they left me alone, and the biggest troublemaker left the company.

Summary

Just 2 generations passed after the Civil Rights Act of 1964 that gave American women, for the first time in USA history, equal opportunity with men. Remarkably, American women succeeded beyond their wildest dreams. Today, they have left men far behind.

Now 60% of American women graduate with college degrees versus 40% of men; more women are employed than men; women have more money than men do, and are more financially savvy; women live 5 years longer than men and know how to take care of themselves and others.

Women created hundreds of organizations, associations, and clubs to support each other and to learn and enlarge their knowledge, information, and skills. They are avid book readers and participate in and support all Public Broadcast Services, PBS.

And how many volunteer organizations to take care of social problems are created, run, financed, supported, and staffed by women? Countless.

Saudi Arabian Women Today

Here is a dramatic example of Saudi Arabian women, who, as of today, live lives of oppression and are treated as merchandize. They also are: "Product of time, place, and circumstances."

Time: The 21 century media news, TV, and internet brought the world into homes of every woman. Saudi Arabian women knew how women in the West and in Muslim countries are living, working, and what rights they have.

Place: Saudi Arabia where women are oppressed and emancipation has not taken place yet. Why? Due to circumstances. In Saudi Arabia, women's rights are defined by government laws, which is Islamic law—Sharia.

In this system, women have no rights.[2] A woman is just a piece of merchandize, and the ownership of a woman passes from one man to another. Women rely on men for their everyday survival. A woman must have a man guardian to give her permission for marriage and divorce;

travel; education; employment; to open a bank account; and miscellaneous jaunts outside her home.

Saudi Arabian women must wear veils covering their bodies from head to toe; voting and driving are forbidden, as are listening to music and answering a telephone.

In summary: Saudi Arabian women are oppressed and have no opportunity for human rights let alone for equal rights with men. They are just caged goods.

Today, there is some movement by activist women for driving rights, which is just a small part in a large sea of Saudi Arabian women oppressions. What a sad and tragic contrast are the lives of Saudi women when compared to their Americans counterparts.

△ △ △

THE MORAL OF THE STORY

A person is a product of time, place, and circumstances, Napoleon Bonaparte concluded in his memoirs. Yes, indeed.

Just compare the dramatic disparity between the lives and achievements of American women versus

Saudi Arabian women. They both are living in the same time, the 20th and the 21st centuries. But they live in different places (the USA versus Saudi Arabia). Under different circumstances (Civil Rights Act of 1964 versus Islamic Sharia law).

And the result is 2 different outcomes: American women's progressive achievement, and Saudi Arabian women's regressive oppression.

American women's stunning achievements have proved that "A person is a product of time, place, and circumstances," When in 1964 the Civil Rights Act was issued and American women were for the 1st time in American history given an equal opportunity with men—wonders happened.

In less than 2 generations American women caught up with their men and today left them behind, in both college education and in financial status. They succeeded beyond anyone's wildest imagination. Today, 60% of American women are graduating with college degrees versus 40% of men.

---

[1] www.biography.com/people/Napoleon

[2] Washington Post "Saudi Arabia's oppression of women goes beyond its ban on driving" by Max Fisher, October 28, 2013.

SHORT STORY

Everything Happens for the Best. Or, Embrace Events and Challenges

△ △ △

Life from time to time gives us threatening challenges to test our endurance, strength, and resilience, as well as our knowledge, information, and skills. Then remunerates us for inflicted wounds and sufferings by changing our destiny for the best.

I). In Shock: I Got Expelled from University

Scanning the Dean's announcement board, prominently displayed on the ground floor of my civil engineering university, I found my name on the list of expelled students from the university.[1] I had suspected this but not expected it.

This news was a traumatic, and I was devastated. I knew the reason. I did not pass my 4th and last math subject, calculus, at the end of the 2nd year. When the fact was, I was the best student in all my math classes, and I tutored students who failed or had difficulties with any math subject. Presently, I had a problem that was beyond my control.

My problem was that in the 4th semester, the professor of my calculus class had a crush on me, on a shy, and timid teenager. His real name was Calafati, and he was also the chairman of the math department.

He probably was in his late 40s, but to me he was as old as my grandfather. I was terrified of him. His crush was so obvious that my class of 400 civil engineering students noticed, and constantly kept joking about it.

One day, at the end of class, the students exited our classroom, and spilled into the empty corridor going to other classes. Standing in the empty corridor was our math professor. Some male students decided he was waiting to see me, and started yelling out so he could hear them: "Alla! Look, your boyfriend is here waiting for you!"

I could only imagine how embarrassed the professor felt. Now he had learned that all students knew about his secret, and were making fun of him by ridiculing him to his face. How could he save his reputation? His solution was to get rid of me, his victim. To him I must be expelled from the university immediately. Soon he had the opportunity to do so, since the spring semester was coming to an end. I had to pass 5 oral exams and 1 written, of which 2 of them were calculus, one written and another oral.

No one could fail me in a written calculus exam, as there was a record of the test. I passed it and was cleared to take the oral calculus exam. In my oral exam, he easily failed me, and there was no record of my answers.

I went to the Dean, who gave me permission and a referral form to take my calculus exam again, this time with any professor of my choice. When I walked into the exam room, a new professor, who did not know me, refused to take my exam once he saw my name, and sent me back to Calafati.

The typical rules were that a student could take an exam with any other professor who teaches the same subject. For me, my sexual harasser, Calafati, changed the rule, and warned all his junior professors not to administer my exam.

Gossip and news spread quickly—even the Dean knew my story—but there was very little he could do to help me. My harasser had a much higher status than my Dean did, and the Dean, for his part, was not going to jeopardize his position for one student, me. I tried once again to take the calculus exam with another professor, but the result was the same; he refused.

Time was not on my side, as the spring semester was over. The fact was, I did not pass the calculus exam, and was expelled from the university. At that time, the phrase "sexual harassment" had not yet been coined, and did not appear in the dictionary.

Despaired, frightened, embarrassed, and disappointed in people, thinking that my life was over and my dream to be a structural engineer was gone forever, as usual, I unloaded my problem onto my paternal grandparents, grandpa Vasily and grandma Anna.

I gave them the inventory of my problems with my calculus professor Calafati, but omitted the reason—his crush on me. I was too ashamed to even utter such words. My noble grandparents would not understand how this old professor could even think about a teenage girl.

After I finished telling them I had been expelled from the university, grandma was already crying, but grandpa, thinking that he misunderstood something, re-questioned me: "You failed a calculus exam?"

He knew that math was my favorite subject, and over the last year he witnessed how I had tutored in our living room several of my male classmates who were behind, or had failed exams. Grandpa was motionless for several minutes, thinking hard.

Next, he disappeared into the living room, found among our important family papers all my school diplomas where I was an honor student, I graduated with 1st degree honors, and put it into his bag. Then he put on a fancy hat, reserved for special occasions, and without saying one word, left the house.

Later I learned in some detail about my grandpa's activities from my former high school friend, who at that time was a personal secretary of the President of my university.

Grandpa went directly to the President. The President stopped all his business and welcomed grandpa into

A Person Is a Product of Time, Place, and Circumstances

his impressive office. In Russia, the most respected and admired people were grandmothers and grandfathers; they were the foundation of every Russian family. That is why when my grandpa asked the secretary to see the President, no questions were asked. In a hurry, the door opened, and he was able to see the President immediately.

Grandpa did not like to make long speeches or beat around the bush. When he talked, all his phrases were short, yet full of wisdom, experienced lessons, or solutions to problems. Here grandpa did the same.

After he introduced himself as a "Grandpa of one of your students," he went directly to the heart of his visit. He placed in front of the President all my honor student academic diplomas and asked him bluntly: "Let me ask you, how my granddaughter, who was always an honor student, has suddenly been expelled from your university?"

The President had no idea but understood where my grandpa was going. He had a great admiration and respect for my grandpa and took off his hat in front of him. Grandpa's son was killed in World War II, and grandpa took it upon himself to raise his son's 2 small children.

On the spot, he issued an order. I was reinstated back to the university into 3rd year evening school. That way, I did not need to face professor Calafati, as there were no more math courses in the 3rd year of university. And later, I could always easily transfer back to the day school if I wanted to.

With this, the President thought that he had solved my problem. But he had not; my problems had just started.

In the fall, I started 3rd year, this time in the evening school. I met my new classmates, made many new friends, and was happy thinking that my nightmare was behind me. Not for the math professor. He did not lose me from his radar and continued focusing on me, determined to save his reputation.

As soon as he learned that the President went over his head for my grandpa, he manufactured a new strategy. This time, every semester, after he scanned the Dean's board and saw what subjects I was taking, without any shame, he would go to every chairman of the department in that particular subject reminding him to weed out bad students, like me, who had failed a calculus exam.

My grades plummeted drastically to C's. Very little I could do since almost all exams were oral. Only occasionally did I receive B's when some curious professors, listening to my perfect answers, were wondering how such an intelligent student was marked as "not very smart, did not pass a calculus exam and should be weeded out."

Such a threatening, hostile, and unfair environment continued for the rest of my study at the university. Having no other alternative and living in constant fear, I kept concentrating on only one dream, I shared with grandpa—to graduate from university, and become a structural engineer.

I suffered tremendously and could not have survived without the full support and encouragement of my classmates. Many of them were my best friends and, being loyal troopers, felt very sorry for me. Usually we studied for each exam in a group of 3–4 students.

The school was very difficult, and many students did not graduate. That was why there were no students drinking, no parties, and almost no dating—we had no time. In my group, all my friends usually received higher grades when mine were always C's, even though I knew the subjects better than the majority of them did.

For the next few years, I took a risk and kept avoiding the final result of my fate with my math professor, instead of facing it at once, hoping that time somehow would cure my problem. It did not. I had just prolonged my agony and my fate until the last year. In the end, I still had to face the music, and take that calculus exam that I had failed in the 4th semester.

The most fearful day of my life, that could change my destiny forever, was coming. To be cleared and admitted to the final level, the final exam, each student must complete all of the school's requirements.

The final exam in engineering universities was to actually design a real life project and then publicly defend this project in front of outside professional engineers, and university professors.

Before that, every student must pass all the courses, assignments, labs, and defend all their lab results. For this, every student received a form from the Dean's office—an inventory, or a list, of all their missed requirements that they must satisfy and pass. On my form, the calculus course in the 4th semester was missing. I could never be cleared to the final level without passing that exam.

The executioner's axe had been hanging over my head during all my previous years at the university. I was aware of it and kept preparing for this exam. How? Constantly keeping my knowledge of calculus fresh by tutoring younger students from 4th year math semesters.

Again, the Dean's office gave me a referral to take the calculus exam with any math professor, not with Calafati. That did not work again. Calafati was a step ahead; he had already issued a warning to all his junior department professors to refer me to him.

The day of my final judgment arrived; the day that could change my life forever.

My 2 best friends and classmates, Alvina and Helen, had slept over in my home the previous night, were supporting me, and then escorted me to my fate. That morning, Calafati was conducting one of his written math exams for his students.

A Person Is a Product of Time, Place, and Circumstances

I walked in, gave him the referral form from the Dean's office, and stood waiting for his orders. He was ready to fail me. To scare me, he put me on display in front of all of his class, ordering me to go to the blackboards where he, in white chalk, on each board wrote 3 problems for me to solve.

I stepped in and quickly started writing the answers. Soon, I populated all 3 blackboards. He was also under some pressure and made a slip-up. He announced that "something here is wrong" and showed the exact area on one of the boards.

I hesitated, not sure about my mistake. Seeing it, he ordered me to take a seat and correct my mistake by solving this particular problem, this time, on paper. I did, and came up with the same answer.

By that time, he cooled down and saw that in both places, on the blackboard and on my paper, my answers were the same, and both were correct. He apologized: "Oh, I am sorry, I missed it."

Then he took the Dean's calculus exam referral, filled it with a B grade, and signed it, indicating that I had passed his exam. I assumed that in front of his class, who witnessed my exam answers, he could not bring himself to risk another embarrassment by failing me again.

I left the room. My friends had already learned that I did well from some of his students who exited his classroom before me, after they had finished their written exam. My friends hugged me, we all cried, and my calculus exam nightmare was over. In the next 6 months, as the final exam, I still needed to design a structural project and then defend it publicly, but that was peanuts.

II). Everything Happens for the Best

Above, in part I). I described my difficult problems associated with the sexual harassment and torture from my math professor, Calafati, which resulted in my being expelled from the university. At the same time, parallel to my university life, I had another part of my life happening.

In another part of my life, destiny stepped in and was remunerating me for my suffering in university. It showered me with unique circumstances, opportunities, and achievements all beyond my wildest imagination.

If someone would tell me to write a fiction script how I would like to see my life and what I wanted to be and achieve, I could not make my fictional life so rewarding and exciting, full of surprises, and bonuses as my real life unfolded at the time.

After I was expelled from the university at the end of my 4th semester, I took a summer job in the accounting department of one factory. There, everyone liked me. I was a shy teenager who respected adults, and put all my energy and will in completing all tasks they gave me.

A Person Is a Product of Time, Place, and Circumstances

There, I met Maria Gredinskaya. She was an economist and a very important person in our city. She worked as a temporary in our factory while waiting for an important position to open up for her in another huge plant. She liked me instantly, and as soon as she left, she invited me to work at her new plant.

I started working there where the person in charge was a legendary chief engineer, Alexander Brimov. He had a staff of many male engineers and his plant was the center of all plant operations. Mr. Brimov was a brilliant engineer, and leader.

The plant operations were like a battlefield; any minute emergency crisis could happen when one of many types of synchronized technologies started malfunctioning, overheated, slowed down, broke down, or stopped producing products.

Engineers who could not solve these problems would run to him. In a few minutes, he would always be able to find the correct solution. He was always surrounded by a group of younger engineers following him everywhere, eager to learn from him. They would act like firefighters running to the center of the action to implement his commands and solutions.

The plant produced reinforced concrete pre-stressed, pre-cast fabricated whole panels for new apartment buildings and condos in the suburbs of Odessa. Odessa was a big metropolitan city with a population over 700,000. The plant was building, actually assembling like cars, new cities—5 story buildings each with 60 to 80 apartments. Panels were arriving from the plant and huge cranes were lifting panels to weld parts together and assemble it into the apartment buildings.

My previous knowledge of strategic planning and accounting helped tremendously to solve many problems that occurred at the plant. Soon, I was given an engineering position, and became the right hand of the chief engineer, Mr. Brimov.

Before I started working at the plant, at the end of each month the chief engineer, Mr. Brimov, and his engineering staff would have to balance the plant's books. They had to give a balance sheet, i.e., input = output, to their headquarters.

In short, all materials brought in by the railways to the plant to fabricate panels for apartment buildings must balance. Material inputs must be equal to the outputs, or to the numbers of the manufactured panels. At the end of the month the engineering staff was working until midnight figuring how to balance the books. To reduce this huge stress, balancing the books was accompanied by a huge consumption of vodka, and smoking cigarettes.

Once I came in, I figured out an easy way to balance their books and took it under my control. Mr. Brimov and his staff were relieved and grateful to me. I had a huge office that became a command post of the plant.

Every day, the engineering staff would gather in my office from where they were commanding all the operations of the plant. Never mind that above my office, they had the whole floor for themselves, each with his own office there.

A myth spread about me that I was the most "intelligent and powerful" person in the plant. The new apartments were at a premium in Odessa. The old city was leveled during World War II and now had 2–3 families that were still living in 1-bedroom apartment.

The war was on Russian soil for 3 years, 26.6 million Russians were killed, and the city of Odessa was ruined. Our plant was building new towns in a suburb of Odessa; some of the buildings among them were condos.

Each condo building had "a commando team" assembled from future condo owners. They sent them to our plant to lobby us—or, in this case lobby me—to schedule the construction of their building ahead of many others.

My job could have become dangerous, if I had a corrupt mind and yielded to accept the huge amounts of cash that were offered to me, often as bribes. But, I was young, idealistic, clean as glass, and was ashamed to roll myself into any dirt, i.e., bribe money. I have kept such an attitude all my life.

My salary was high; I paid no rent, food, or utilities to my grandparents, and hence saved a huge amount of money. I bought a condo for myself, paid in full.

In short, for me everything happened for the best, even with a life changing event such as getting expelled from the university after the 4th semester. If I had not been expelled and finished university with all my former classmates, by law, I would be sent for 2 years to far away places from Odessa, across the Soviet Union.

Where my qualification was needed, and not where I wanted to work. In the USSR, or the Soviet Union, university education was free, student housing and books were all free, and students received a small stipend for other expenses, such as buying food and clothing.

The majority of my former classmates received assignments in Siberia. No one ever received assignments in Odessa; here, competition for engineering jobs was tough in one of the most beautiful metropolitan cities in the country. And of course, none of my former classmates were able to buy a condo before graduation, like I did; they had no money, were all living off the government's small stipend, and were not in charge of condos construction like I was.

At the beginning, I was the most unlucky among all my former university classmates. I had been given horrifying challenges, for reasons beyond my control, and I was expelled from the university, described in detail in part I) above. This event was the lowest point in my young life.

Then, fate interfered and remunerated me for all my suffering and showered me with unique opportunities. My grandpa reinstated me back to my university, and I had a dream engineering position with a big salary, especially for a teenager who just started her 3rd year in university.

Before I graduated from university, I bought a condo and paid for it in full from my big engineering salary savings. As soon as I graduated and received my life's dream, a diploma in civil engineering, I was promoted again. This time, I started working in the center of the city in the plant's headquarters. Also, I moved out from my grandparents' apartment into my brand new condo. All my life's dreams were fulfilled in just 4 years, all beyond my wildest imagination.

But I missed my old job on the "floor" at the plant: its excitement, stress, and crises; working there was like being on a battlefield. The plant staff missed me too. There was no one with my knowledge to balance the plant books at the end of each month. They were having problems at the plant and expanded my position to 4 engineers and made it a "Construction Assembly Department."

That did not solve their problems. Mr. Brimov and his engineering staff were again under stress, not knowing if the monthly books would be balanced correctly. They could face criminal charges if an audit found that a lot of the materials had not been accounted for.

Mr. Brimov left the plant and assumed another chief engineering position, this time on the construction side, and many of his engineers did the same. Unfortunately, 4 years later, he died suddenly from pneumonia complications; he was in his mid-40s.

By that time I was working in Tanzania, East Africa, and my grandmother and my friend Maria Gridinskaya gave me this sad news. In her letter, she described Mr. Brimov's funeral: "Imagine what a legend Alexander Brimov was when the whole city of Odessa come to his funeral and stopped the city traffic!

"His casket was carried by his admirers on their shoulders from his home to the cemetery; there was a big band following his casket, playing sad music; then hundreds of baskets of flowers followed; and then a procession made up of the crowd of many thousands."

That was a very sad day for me. My grandparents and I were very grateful to Mr. Alexander Brimov. He took responsibility for me, believed in me, and gave me an opportunity—a huge responsibility and highly paid engineering position to just a 3rd year engineering student. I learned from him and his staff how to solve any problem; they molded my character into a stoic, fearless, honest, straightforward, no lies, no manipulations; risk taker—who can stand up to anyone, with nothing to hide or be afraid off.

△ △ △

THE MORAL OF THE STORY

Everything happens for the best. Embrace life's challenges do not be afraid of them. They all happen for the best. From time to time, life throws us a curveball, or ambushes us with dangerous challenges—all on purpose.

This is to test our endurance and resilience so we can learn new skills to survive under circumstances, and events that are beyond our control.

Then fate will intervene almost immediately, and for all our suffering, struggles, and inflicted wounds, it remunerates us with many bonuses that in turn will change our destiny for the best.

The challenges we're given are given to us for a special purpose—to grow. Challenges change our lives; we become stoic, resilient, honest, sophisticated, and better people with new skills and improved quality of lives.

---

[1] All Russian university courses were 5 years in length; Americans university courses are 4 years. Russian high schools are 10 years in length not 12 as in the USA, but they were very difficult, 6 days per week; only one break, during the New Year. All exams were oral and written. No multiple choice questions. All exams were taken by teachers from other schools, so students' teachers could not exaggerate grades or pass students who were not up to par in subjects. Russian students finish high school at age 16, and graduate from university at age 21.

#3 SHORT STORY

Self-Esteem and Maslow's Theory. Or, an Elephant and a Poodle

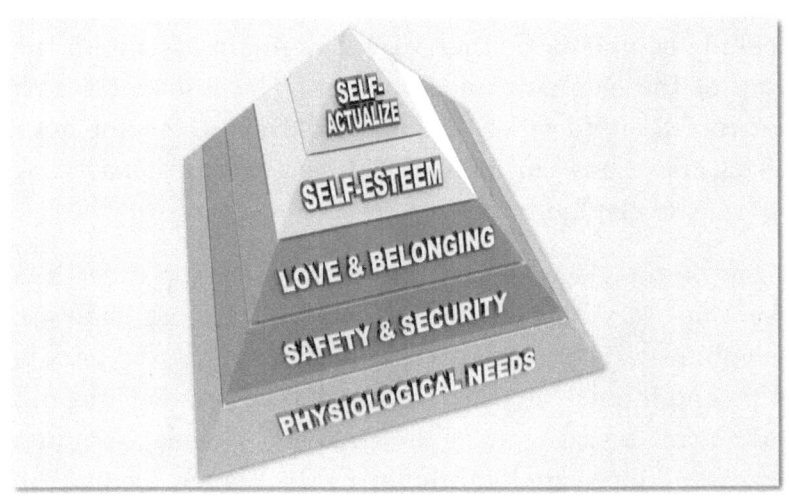

△ △ △

Self-esteem, or, this riddle "An Elephant and a Poodle" I learned in my primary school in a language class book that consisted of many stories. The stories were teaching children wisdom and everyday skills. This story actually was written as a poem.

An Elephant and a Poodle

A circus came to the city. Big animals, elephants, were transported by foot from a railway station to the center of the city where the circus was located. The elephant handlers were parading elephants along the city streets in a chain.

Stretched in straight line, elephants were walking calmly behind each other, each holding in his mouth the tail of the elephant ahead of him. The unusual march attracted city dwellers, adults, children, and some dogs. A big crowd lined up along the streets to see the marching parade of elephants.

One of the dogs in the crowd, a French poodle, had become very agitated upon seeing the big majestic elephants. He ran after the last elephant in the parade line and intensively, as a ringing bell, began barking out of control, trying to scare the elephant. The elephant just kept walking, completely ignoring the French poodle. The elephant's indifference provoked the poodle into more excitable actions.

Next, he began jumping up and down barking at a higher pitched volume. Nothing. No reaction from the elephant. The elephant kept walking, staying his course, and the French poodle kept barking.

After we finished reading this poem, our teacher probed us with a question: "What does this story teach you?" Students tried giving diverse answers.

The teacher explained: "An elephant has very high self-esteem; he is confident and sure of himself and is focusing on what he is supposed to do: walk in a straight line with other elephants throughout busy city streets, not to get hurt, not to hurt others, and ignore the poodle.

"At the same time, a little French poodle has very low self-esteem. The poodle barks at a big elephant, thinking that all people, children, and other dogs around him would think that he is very tough, because the small poodle is barking at the big elephant."

She offered even more interpretation of the story: "The story teaches you to have high self-esteem, confidence in yourself. You must be strong and focus on your main goal and not be distracted by something else that is not important to you."

Next, to visualize what she meant by her definition of self-esteem and how self-esteem applies to real life, she gave us a familiar example.

"For example, today after school, you are going to start your homework. It is not going to be an easy task for you with all the surrounding distractions.

"You hear from open windows some children are playing soccer outside, others are jumping rope, your little sister in another room is playing the piano, the family dog keeps running from one room to another, a telephone is ringing, and many more. As you can see, there are many amusements to derail your focus from doing your homework.

"Do you have confidence in yourself and have high self-esteem? Are you as strong as the elephant and are you going to ignore all distractions around you and continue focusing on only one goal, your homework? Or are you weak, as the French poodle is, and are going to react to amusements, give up on your homework and join your sister, or run outside to play? If you do, there would be many consequences to your low self-esteem actions.

"If you do not finish your homework, the next day you could receive an "F." Once you have failing grades, you are going to repeat the same class the next year, when all your friends will be in a higher grade.

"Even more, your mind is going to be empty. It will not have enough knowledge and information to solve all your problems as you are growing up and becoming a young adult.

"All your current actions have many consequences. If you have low self-esteem, you are going to finish school with low grades and your life later will become stressful and difficult."

Our teacher scared many of us. I remembered the self-esteem story and my teacher's interpretation of it many years later when I took an economics class in my civil engineering university.

Maslow's Theory: the 5 Steps Hierarchy of Human Needs and Development

In my economics class, we learned about Maslow's theory: the 5 steps hierarchy of human needs and development. It echoed the self-esteem in the short story "The Elephant and the Poodle" from my language class before. Abraham Maslow interpreted the theory of human development as being a pyramid of the "Hierarchy or Needs" or "A Theory of Human Motivation."

In our economics book, the Maslow theory was interpreted by a visual picture of a young woman climbing 5 steps.

The last step, #5, was the happiest step. Smiling, she was standing on the step proclaiming: "I am on the self-actualization step!" Abraham Maslow postulated that the 5 steps in his "Hierarchy of Needs" are all produced by people's needs, and motivation. When a person's 1st step is satisfied, he can start concentrating on the next step.

The 1st step is—the most fundamental, basic physical needs: food, water, shelter, and clothing.

The 2nd step is—security needs: physical safety assuring you are not in any physical danger and have economic stability.

The 3rd step is—social needs: have family, belong to a group, and be loved.

The 4th step is—self-esteem: confidence, prestige, and respect.

The 5th step is—the most advanced, it is where a person grows into noble traits of character; having dignity, honor, and morality; high creativity, problems solving abilities; treating everyone equally, doing great things for others.

On this self-actualization step, a person has reached such a level of personal and intellectual development that he is looking how to help others and society. It becomes a higher calling for her or him.

Each of the 5 steps needs a motivational factor, as a red thread going from one step to the next one.

A Person Is a Product of Time, Place, and Circumstances

We students loved the Maslow theory and soon, my best friends and I, started claiming that we already had reached the "self-actualization" step.

We reasoned that by this time in our lives, each of us had read hundreds classic books written by world famous classical writers. We saw numerous movies, the majority of them international, and went to the theater many times to hear the most popular operas, saw ballet performances, not to mention visits to the drama theatre, the circuses, and philharmonic classical music performances, all from a young age.

And our summers? We spent weekends on the beach reading books, swimming, playing volleyball, and discussing various popular topics and trends. Evenings we spent dancing to the world's most popular rock-and-roll, and rushing to buy tickets for many international concerts and sporting events that were going on in our city. We believed that we knew everything and had already climbed the 4 previous steps.

In summary: A wise riddle "An Elephant and a Poodle" teaches self-esteem using a visual example. How the elephant, who had very high self-esteem, kept marching to his destination, and ignored completely the obnoxious barking at him of the French poodle. Meanwhile, the French poodle, who had very low self-esteem caused a commotion by jumping up and down barking at the elephant. The French poodle sought attention in expecting that others around her (people, children, and other dogs) would think that she was very brave if she was barking at such a mammoth animal, as the elephant was.

Abraham Maslow's self-esteem theory has 5 steps, a "Hierarchy of Needs" (food and shelter, safety, social, self-esteem, and self-actualization) and was created based on people's needs, and motivation.[1]

In his theory, people are advancing their intellect from one step to the next step only after their needs are satisfied in the previous step. In other words, life is the progress, moving ahead. Do not stay stationary on the same step.

Self-actualization is the 5th step, the highest step of intellectual human development. Here, dignity, honor, morality, no prejudice, care about the society and others, and creativity to solve problems on a larger scale are the major traits of human character.

Once a person reaches the self-actualization step, only the sky is the limit; he can do and achieve many great things. When on the 5th step, self-actualization, he becomes a contributor to society.

Question

Why did my poor meager life in Kinondoni, Tanzania, shock Miss Frica (an English lady who was giving me English lessons) to such an extent, that she decided that it was beneath her status to associate with me, a person with a low status who was the only white woman living in a black neighborhood in Kinondoni? At the same time, why did I not even notice my poor meager status when living in Kinondoni?

Answer

Before, I was living in Odessa, the most beautiful metropolitan city, which some foreign tourists think is more beautiful than Paris. I graduated from civil engineering university, was working in main headquarters of the engineering company.

I bought a new contemporary condo paid in full by cash, read hundreds world classic books, saw many of international movies, operas, ballet, dramas, circuses, concerts, traveled to many cities, got married, and had a child.

Then I went to post-colonial Africa to help build their superstructure and all that before the age of 26. As per Maslow's theory, I was on the 5th and highest step, self-actualization, when I went to Tanzania.[2]

At the same time, Miss Frica, an British lady, was living in Tanzania, Dar es Salaam, for a long time (Tanzania was a former British colony), was a spinster, never was married, was a nurse, and was promoted as an assistant to the director of a nursing school. She lived in a big mansion, on the Indian Ocean, and had an old

Volkswagen Beetle. I assumed she was on the 3rd step in Maslow's hierarchy of needs—social needs.

That is why she was so concerned with her social status. Once she saw how poor I was, she stopped associating with me, as I was a person of low status. When, 1 year later, my status changed above hers, she became very jealous of me. Her traits of character were selfishness, to satisfy her personal needs and not to help others.

△ △ △

THE MORAL OF THE STORY

A wise riddle "An Elephant and a Poodle," teaches self-esteem using a visual example. The elephant has a high self-esteem. The French poodle has a low self-esteem, indeed no self-esteem.

Self-esteem is very important for human development and Maslow developed a theory about it, a "Hierarchy of Needs." His theory has 5 steps of needs: basic, safety, social, self-esteem, and self-actualization.

Self-actualization is the highest step of human development when creativity, innovations, and problem solving flourish and a person elevates himself above his personal need, and start serving others.

To reach the 5th step, one must develop his or her personal intellect by reading scores of books and learning everyday from everything, and from everybody.

Every person you meet who is better or knows more, do not get jealous; instead, envy this person and make him or her your mentor—learn from them. Read, learn, study, travel and see new places, visit foreign countries, and dream to become a better person, like your heroes.

---

[1] http://en.wikipedia.org/wili/Maslow/s-hierararchuy_of_needs

[2] Please read another short story #7 in book 1: "What Is Happiness? Or, What Were the Happiest Years in Your Life?"

Please read another story in this book: "Risk: to Take, or Not to Take? Or, Once You Take a Risk Your Probability of Success Goes from 0% to 50%."

SHORT STORY

**Risk: to Take or Not to Take?
Or, Once You Take a Risk,
Your Probability of Success Goes
from 0% to 50%**

A Person Is a Product of Time, Place, and Circumstances

△ △ △

At the beginning of the 1970s, there were not many women engineers in the USA. Even brilliant women pioneers who graduated from the top engineering schools were lucky to find secretarial jobs in engineering companies.

It was during this time, I arrived in the USA from the Soviet Union via Africa. Naive, young, and idealistic, I saw the world as a rose garden. I answered a newspaper advertisement and got a job as a structural engineer to design bridges.

Why did the company hire me and not an American woman engineer? There was a reason for that. Later, I learned that the top management at the company wanted to see the differences between Russian and American engineers. During the Cold War between the USA and the USSR, American engineers paid very close attention to Russian engineering and scientific developments.

In my first 3–4 days on the job, I familiarized myself with their structural design requirements by reading 2 volumes of the federal and state codes, requirements, and regulations for structural designs.

Soon after, a chief engineer called me into his office and made an announcement in front of his 3–4 department managers. They had decided that I was going to design a 3-span reinforced concrete bridge over Ramp A, all on my own; L.R. 795, 3-span composite prestressed concrete I-beam bridge.[1] He unrolled a construction field drawing on his desk. Then, he took a red marker pen and drew a curved line between 2 points. That was an approximate location of the bridge. At each end of the bridge line, he added a corresponding letter, A and B. That was it.

A line in red pen indicating a 3-span bridge in the air from point A to point B over Ramp A. No examples of other drawings and calculations were given to me, and no guidance or instructions on how to design it. Silence fell over the room, indicating the meeting was over.

As I took the rolled up field drawing into my hands, timidly, I started walking toward my station when I unexpectedly became dizzy and nauseous. My brain was searching frenetically for a solution and milling through my mind. How in the world was I going to design this bridge? Only a miracle could do it.

Before, when working in the Soviet Union, I was designing and assembling pre-cast, pre-stressed apartments. Then I left and worked in Africa, where my specialty skills were reinforced concrete buildings, using the metric systems, European design, and all in French.

Engineers, as with all other professionals, usually specialized in different structures: roads, buildings, bridges, subways, dams, and graving docks. Now, overnight, the company had changed my specialty from buildings to bridges and left me alone to succeed or fail.

I had another huge problem—all the men engineers were offended that the company had hired a woman to design the bridge. They were sure that from now on their profession was going downhill. That created a hostile work environment, with these engineers angry and spiteful towards me.

For the rest of the day, I looked at the field drawing, searching for ideas on how to design the bridge. I came up with nothing.

In my engineering school, not one professor had even mentioned the word "bridge." In school, I took general engineering subjects: math, physics, chemistry, strength of materials, and many more. Only once on the job would engineers specialize and learn how to design different structures.

That is why this bridge was the challenge of a lifetime. Fear, despair, doubt, low self-esteem, and suffering were all emotions that bombarded my mind. I knew very well that if no breakthrough occurred and I could not design the bridge—then my engineering career would be over. No one was ever going to hire me as an engineer again. My childhood dream to be a structural engineer could end abruptly. My career, profession, life, and destiny were all on the line.

Excuses and ways out crept into my thoughts. If I left the company, no one could blame me: I was a woman;

my specialty was buildings in the metric system and in European design; I had never designed a bridge before.

No American woman engineer had ever designed a bridge by herself; I was a foreigner in a new country and English was a new language for me; I had 2 small children; and my husband was a physician and here, in the USA, wives of physicians did not work.

At the end of the day, I took a detour on my way to picking up my children from their babysitter. I stopped by a bridge to see what it looked like underneath. I saw decks, beams, girders, piers, columns, and foundations. The next morning when I drove across the bridge, I looked left and right and saw parapets; then I noticed that every 400–600 feet, my car kept jumping. That was due to joints between the spans, I thought.

That morning, when I arrived to my office, I had already learned a lot about a bridge. Randomly, on the field drawing around the prominent red line indicating the location of "the bridge," I sketched a dozen soil borings and went to the soil department asking them to find out the soil pressure under each boring.

They took me seriously and asked how soon I needed the soil pressure results. My self-esteem shot through the roof. I was exited—I was on the right track!

Here, on the spot, I made a decision. I was going to take the risk! I was not going to give up and leave, as I had thought just yesterday. Instead, I was going to stay on and try to design this bridge until the company found out that I did not know how to design it, and fired me.

Once I made the decision to take the risk and keep on trying to design the bridge, my probability[2] of success went up from 0% to 50%! Now there were 2 potential outcomes, I had a 50/50 chance at success or failure. Yesterday, before I committed myself to the attempt, my odds were 0%.

Today I took a risk and changed my destiny! I became fearless and found a solution—I need to design each part of the bridge separately. Then put all the parts together, as in a jigsaw puzzle. If they fit, it would become the bridge! I was on the right track.

Using common sense and logic then applying math, physics and strength of materials I invented calculations and drawings for each part of the bridge from scratch. Then I put all the designed parts together—so they fit as a glove. That is how I designed this, my 1st bridge.

Attempt to Delete My Name as the Single Designer of the Bridge

But, there was no smooth sailing ahead, nothing went perfectly easy. Soon I faced another dilemma. I was forced to make a risky decision and stand up to my manager, Mr. Shepak, in order to keep my project and my self-esteem. After I found the solution on how to design the bridge, I put my heart and mind into it and the bridge design was progressing quickly.

Then, when I had designed almost all the parts of the bridge and was leading up to the last part, the foundation, Mr. Shepak got jealous and attempted to push me out of the bridge project and erase my name as the bridge designer.

One day, unexpectedly, without any warning, he appeared in front of me demanding that I must wrap up all my drawings and calculations and give them all to Jerry, his protégée. "Jerry will finish designing it," he declared.

I was speechless. In a fraction of a second, I recognized his intentions. I did not accept his trick. I stood up to him and said: "This is my bridge, I already finished designing more than 90% of it, and I am now starting the design the last part of it, the foundation. I am not going to give it to Jerry. I will finish it myself." Mr. Shepak did not like it, but there was very little he could do.

From the beginning, Mr. Shepak had been a trouble maker. He hated me and would have done anything to get rid of me. You see, I learned that from the start he was opposed to hiring me. Some months before me, there had been an American woman engineer who applied to this company. But, Mr. Shepak rejected her resume and did not even answer her.

When I applied, this time top management had decided that they wanted to see the difference between Russian

A Person Is a Product of Time, Place, and Circumstances

and American engineers and did not listen to Mr. Shepak's objections.

Once I was hired, Mr. Shepak started watching and needling me constantly. He continued his underhanded tricks to make me look bad and flounder, and was plotting to get rid of me. It was he, who recommended to a chief engineer that I should design the entire bridge alone, on my own. He even asked his friend, a chief engineer, to assign me to his department. That way, he had "supreme power over me" and never gave me any examples or guidance on how to design the bridge.

He wanted me to fail. Despite these obstacles I had succeeded and almost finished the bridge design, so he invented another scheme to undermine me.

To erase my achievement, he attempted to take my almost completed bridge design and give it to his protégée. In reality, Jerry would have designed only the foundation of the bridge, but his name, not mine, would be displayed prominently on all the drawings of the bridge. That way I would become invisible; my name would have disappeared forever from the bridge.

Still I was not out of the woods, my bridge must be checked and accepted by the company. I was 100% sure that my bridge was correct; I made not 1 error.

A team of engineers was assembled to check my bridge. (Usually, a company would not put all their eggs into one basket. Typically a bridge is designed by a team of engineers each specializing in a particular part of the structure: decks, parapets, beams, girders, piers, columns, and foundations.)

Then, approximately 1 hour later, the team called me stating that they had never seen such calculations and drawings before. I stood up and fought back. In a high-pitched voice I expressed my intention and reminded them about theirs: "Look guys, you did not give me your calculations and drawings to follow, you wanted me to fail.

"So I invented my own from scratch. They are simple, a child can understand. Why can't you? Do not change my design! If you do not understand something, just ask me. There is not 1 error here." It worked!

After 3 months they finished checking my bridge and accepted it 100%. My bridge became a standard in the company. The company was so impressed that they started looking for another woman engineer. The rest is history.

After my bridge success and acceptance by my peers, Mr. Shepak's bullying intensified, and, in the end I decided to leave the company. But my achievement and my name remain on the bridge despite his best efforts.

Question

Why had I panicked, went into despair, and my self-esteem suddenly dropped to the bottom when I was assigned to design my 1st bridge, the whole bridge alone?

Answer

Scared of the unknown, I had never designed a bridge before. I was frightened that my engineering career would be over if I could not design this bridge; the world was closing in, and I was desperate.

The next day, I stepped on the right track when an idea came to me that I needed to measure the soil pressure under the bridge.

My low self-esteem disappeared, and my adrenaline shot up high which propelled me from the bottom step back to my 5th step—self-actualization, as per Maslow's theory.

My creativity sprinted back into action, solving my problems and inventing calculations and drawings from scratch.

My personal development, as per Maslow's theory, "5 steps of Hierarchy," was already on the 5th step before the bridge design. Then the bridge design project, for a few days, pushed me down to the bottom, on the 1st step.

Once I found a solution to my problem (I needed soil pressure under the bridge) my resurrected self-esteem elevated me back to the top, the 5th step.

This low event in my life changed my life and destiny. I continued progressing forward, nothing stopped, or derailed me.

△ △ △
THE MORAL OF THE STORY

Take a risk, life is full of risks. The above clearly demonstrates how I took a risk and designed my 1st bridge alone and it changed my destiny. Risk: To take or not to take?

Always take a risk, a risk that is under your control. Under your control means the risk is dependent on you and not on other people.

Once you make a decision to take a risk, your probability of success immediately increases from 0% to 50%. The odds of success are 50/50. Risks can change your life and destiny. If you are afraid to take a risk from the start, if you procrastinate, and are unsure of yourself—still go ahead and take a risk.

If you don't, many years later you will always be wondering and asking yourself, "If I had taken that risk and succeeded, how different would

A Person Is a Product of Time, Place, and Circumstances

both my destiny and life be today? I would be a different person and perhaps would lived in different places." You never know until you go out and take a risk. Without a risk your probability of success is ="0", or zero.

Life is a risk. You take risks every day that you don't even notice. For example, as soon as you start driving, you are taking a risk (a risk that is beyond your control). There are many irresponsible drivers on the road who are drunk, on drugs, texting, talking on a cellular phone, or speeding. Any one of them could hit your car. You are risking your life driving every day. Every year there are over 10 million car accidents in the USA and over 35,000 fatalities.

Yet all other types of risks do not involve risking your life (as everyday driving does). Do you understand my point? What do you have to lose by pushing yourself in some other aspect of your life?

Take new assignments, get a new job, find mentors, read motivational and informational books, create ideas, implement your dream, or get involved in a new relationship. Invest in yourself and became sophisticated:[3] take courses, always read new books, read at least some of the "100 best classic books ever written," watch the best classic movies that were ever produced. From there, start imitating your heroes. Act, behave, dress, and speak as if you were "them" and good things will happen. You will become sophisticated with high self-esteem. You will stand out in the crowd and everyone will notice you.

Chase and expand your education: take classes, read many books, get mentors, listen to new people, and learn new information and knowledge from them.

The brain is a muscle; if you do not use it, you will lose it. Travel to foreign countries and change your point of view. Be in love with life. From a safe zone of 0% get into the risky zone of a 50/50 shot and give yourself the chance to change your life and destiny.

---

[1] "Prestressed concrete is a method for overcoming concrete's natural weakness in tension. It can be used to produce beams, floor, or bridges with a longer span than is practical with ordinary reinforced concrete" en wikipedia.org/wiki/prestressed-concrete

[2] Probability is a theory; expressed in a parentage (%). It deals with uncertainty. Probability measures the chance that something will happened out of a number of possible outcomes. Example, a coin toss has a probability of 50%. It is equally likely it will land on either side – heads or tails – with each flip of the coin.

[3] Dictionary defined sophisticated person characteristics as: able to interpret complex issues, experienced, enlightened, knowledgeable, good tests and manners – all altered by education and experience.

Please read another story in this book "Self-Esteem and Maslow's Theory. Or, an Elephant and a Poodle."

Please read in Book 3 of the trilogy 3 stories: "Skills Are Transferable from One Industry to Another"; "How to Design Innovations"; and "Learn New Skills Here: How to Solve External and Internal Problems."

#5 SHORT STORY

Everything Has a Limit. Or, How Much Stress Can Our Brain and Body Take?

△ △ △

It is common knowledge that if we injure, or wound ourselves, the area starts bleeding, our body system immediately sounds an emergency alert and diminishes all other body functions and runs, as an ambulance rescue team, to stop the bleeding. It then shifts into recovery mode, rushing nutrients to the injured area to soothe, and to start the recovery process. That is how our body system survival defenses functions.

But what happens to our brain and our mind when we are faced with a difficult, or sometimes impossible intellectual task that vexes and challenges our brain subjecting it to stress and pressure?

What happens when we face a life-threatening event or career-changing situation and must solve extraordinary problems or find an instant solution?

Here, I am sure the same analogy, as in a bleeding cut on our body, applies to our brain as well. Let's see how our brain reacts and endure an excessive amount of stress, and pressure from my own real life examples.

Learning English in 4 Months

When I learned English in 4 months I encountered for the 1st time in my life an unbearable stressful event. From the beginning, I knew that I was a bad linguist, as it had taken me many years to learn French.

A Person Is a Product of Time, Place, and Circumstances

After graduating from the university, I went to work in Africa in Rwanda, a French speaking country, and then we (my then husband Chrys and our 10-month-old son) encountered a life-threatening event in Rwanda and escaped via Kenya to Dar es Salaam, the capital city of neighboring Tanzania.

The problem was that Tanzania was a former British colony, and the official language was English which I did not know. Chrys, who knew English very well, started his internship for physicians, and was working and living in the hospital 24/7.

I was living alone with a toddler, and was cut off from my work and from life. To improve my life, I had to learn English and find a job. I had no other choice or alternative. There were English courses at the university, but it would take 1–2 years going that route.

Impatient and in a hurry, I designed a crude method for teaching myself English from 6 a.m. to midnight. Like a robot, I kept reading, memorizing, and repeating each word many times, and then reading whole sentences again and again.

At the end of the 4th month, I mastered English, but an unforeseen event stopped and derailed my progress briefly. One afternoon, suddenly I became very dizzy and nauseous and fainted.

When I regained consciousness everything around me was wobbling and circling as if I was on a fast-spinning merry-go-round. From such a fast speed I was throwing up, and had many blackouts. It was painful and I was frightened to be alive. Chrys brought me to a central hospital, Muhimbili, in Dar es Salaam.

A team of European physicians examined me and concluded from my symptoms that I had a brain cancer. I was in the hospital for 4–5 days, a time which remains bleary in my memory.

All I remember was spinning into a deep, dark hole 100s of time, and preying to spin back into the light of the room again. Unexpectedly, I recovered. The spinning was gone, as was the dizziness, nausea, and vomiting. I stood up and did not pass out. As if by the supernatural, it appeared I was cured; only my body's weakness and slight nausea remained.

In less than a week, my strength was back, and my body was ready to face life's new challenges again.

Why had I suddenly recovered in the hospital after 4–5 days? Later, thinking about it, I attributed it to the rest and nutritious food. In the hospital, the stress on my brain was alleviated. It was not bombarded for hours memorizing and repeating without stopping new words and phrases again and again.

I was lying in the hospital bed, 24/7, hooked to an IV device feeding nutrients and medication into my body, I almost used no energy, just for small movements during the physicians' examinations, and the IV drip was nourishing my brain with nutrients.

That time, my only objective was to learn English as soon as possible, get a job, and get back into the life that was passing me by. I did not dwell on this life-threatening horrible episode, but instead forgot about it and moved forward. The following week, I got my 1st job and the rest was history. But, what was it? Why had my brain suddenly shutdown and nearly collapsed?

The answer come to me years later when for the 2nd time, the same exact life-threatening episode visited my brain out of the blue again, but under somewhat different circumstances.

Designing a Graving Dock

In the USA, I quit the company that I liked very much. I could not continue working under my boss who was making my life unbearable.

From the beginning, he was angry that against his advice the company hired me, and that I was the 1st woman engineer in the company. He was doing everything to sabotage me and prove that he was right, and that I did not belong there. I thought that a new company could solve my problems. Just the opposite happened, and it was as if I had jumped from the frying pan into a raging fire.

During my interview with a new company, all top management were great to me, especially my future boss and head of the department. The company got a contract from South Korea, to build a graving dock for their ships' repairs and maintenance.

What is a graving dock? A graving dock is built near coastal water for the repair, maintenance, and construction of new ships; a graving dock has blocks, walls, and gates. A gate opens for ships to come in. It then closed, and water was pumped out of the dock, readying the ship for repair or maintenance.

In this case, the problem was how to design a huge metal gate which could open and close, as an aerial lift bridge, vertically into the air. The manager who got this contract was promoted, a new graving dock department was created and he was put in charge of it. But, he had a problem—neither he, nor anyone in his department knew how to design a metal gate, in this case an aerial lift gate.

That was the reason he was so great during my interview, encouraging me to accept the position. Little did I know that I would be solely responsible for designing the aerial lift gate, something I had never done before and had no clue how to design.

Once I was in, he changed 180 degrees. He became hostile towards me putting me on the rock and board, forcing me to find a solution on how to design the gate, and then to design it.

All male engineers and technicians in the department followed his lead by being equally hostile towards me, their jobs depended on what I produce, and could deliver. In desperation, he and other top managers flew to Japan and took hundreds of pictures of comparable Japanese aerial lift gates in graving docks and gave it to me.

Well, photos of Japanese gates made no difference for me. I had to face reality and invent a gate design for this South Korean project. Could I invent the aerial lift gate or not? In the end, my mind was under such pressure to produce results, that I found the solution. I then proceeded to design about 70% of the gate.

Then, one Sunday, when I was sunning with my children at the swimming pool, suddenly I started experiencing dizziness, nausea, and vertigo. I came home thinking that I had probably a heat stroke.

No chance. My symptoms intensified, and I was admitted to the hospital where I could not move on my own and was shuffled through many tests. The diagnosis was that I probably had a brain tumor.

At the same time, those symptoms were so familiar to me. Where had I had them before? Oh, yes, years before when I was living in Tanzania, Africa, and pushed myself to the extreme, when I learned English in 4 months and got a job.

I recognized that I had no brain tumor. I had succumbed to a brain breakdown with the tremendous weight of stress I put on myself by inventing the aerial lift gate from scratch—it was that stress and demand that was tormenting my brain and my mind; my mind cannot endured it any longer such 24/7 constant stress.

I concluded that I must quit this job. As soon as I was discharged from the hospital and felt better, I resigned without giving the company 2 weeks notice. The department scrambled and was in disarray after my resignation, but I did not care.

Later, I learned that, shortly after my resignation, the department was closed, and the department chief left the company.

Designing a Spiral for Baltimore's Subway

My colleagues surrounded me, asking: "How? How did you do it?" Speedily, I swept my mind, trying to retrieve a quick and simple answer for them, but came up with nothing.

They continued lingering for a while, with great anticipation for the formulas I invented to design "a spiral" for Baltimore's subway. (Subway has 2 types of structures: aerial above the ground, and a tunnel below the ground.) "I do not know," I said honestly. They were in disbelief. Disappointed, one by one they left. Indeed, how did I invent formulas to design "a spiral" for 3.5 miles of Baltimore subway's aerial structure?

That is how. Déjà vu again. It was a nightmare I could not forget in a hurry. It all started when a company won a federal contract for millions of dollars to design 3.5 miles of aerial structure for Baltimore's subway.

They hired 3 floors of engineering and administrative personnel in a high-rise building. That was the easy part. The difficult part was the fact that they had no idea how to design "a spiral." Advertising in engineering journals across the country in search of engineers who could design "a spiral" failed to solve their problem.

They received no reply. No one knew how to design it, and no one wanted to risk their career in a failed attempt at designing it.

The company was in hot water. Would the company end up closing? Then, one of the chief engineers found the solution—he hired me and assigned me to design it.

Recently, I had finished the design of a 10-span bridge and 4 ramps over the Patapsco River, I-95, in downtown Baltimore, all alone, one person, and he thought that I could probably design "a spiral." I had no alternative but to design it, or my career would be over.

I started from a blank sheet—I had no clue or idea. He told me that in the Library of Congress in Washington, D.C. there were 2 books written in French about the recent design of Paris' new subway.

The company got those books and I read them (I knew French well). But the books were not about "a spiral" design, rather about the philosophy, problems, and approach to design. Plus, Paris is not Baltimore. There was a European design, and there were no mention of a spiral there. I was at square one.

What Is a Spiral for a Subway Aerial Structure?

Aerial structure is something built suspended above ground, an example of which is a bridge. Everyone is familiar with spirals or curves on highways, when a relatively straight line highway bends into a spiral in some parts. Drivers slow down when driving on a curve. Why? To accommodate a 4,000 pound car's inertia and acceleration forces that are pulling it to drive in a straight line and off the curve.

There is no problem in designing a curve on a highway, and many civil engineers know how to design it. Millions of miles of highways were built in the USA and hundreds of thousands of road spirals were designed.

As for a subway spiral? Not many structural engineers know how to design "a spiral" for a subway aerial structure. Why?

A Person Is a Product of Time, Place, and Circumstances

Not many new subways in the USA are built. A spiral for a subway must accommodate a train with many subway cars, which has an approximate weight of 1,000,000 pounds in total. Let's imagine the inertia and acceleration forces of such mass generates when it is trying to pull the train to run in a straight line, and jumping down from the bridge.

Even more, subways are located in populated areas where there are many other existing structures already in place, and a subway train must snake around them. A spiral length is for tight twists and turns, leaving no room for any errors.

That is why and how the next 4 months were pure hell. My mind was racing without stopping, searching for a solution. I barely slept from constant head pains and rushes of adrenaline.

Never before had I suffered so much as a human being. During this time period, 2 times I woke up in the morning and a razor sharp thought passed through my mind—I wish I did not wake up; to be alive was so painful!

I brushed aside the terrifying thoughts, remembering that I woke up to fulfill my immediate morning duties and prepare the children for schools. For the next 30–40 minutes, I took care of my children and placed my personal problems on the back burner; then it was time for me to rush to my office, and my day started.

My tormentor, a chief engineer, was similarly in bad situation, as his job, prestige, self-esteem, and position were on the line. It was he, who was the architect, in charge of pushing the company to compete for the bid to design the subway, and now he could not deliver the design. So, he resorted to pressuring me to achieve what he could not.

Every morning, before going to his floor above, he would stop at my desk to needle me, as if it was he, not I, who was doing everyone favor: "Do you think you can design a spiral?" he asked me plaintively.

I was not leaving the office every evening until late, after 10:00 p.m. or 11:00 p.m. My parking was in the center of downtown Baltimore under Charles Plaza. It was scary to walk, as the streets were empty. I met only ladies of the night, and occasional police with their German Shepherd dogs.

In the end I found the solution, an innovation on how to design a spiral. I designed one spiral span all by hand, but there were over 550 more spans; it could take a long time, years, or an army of engineers to design them all by hand. To speed up a design, a computer program was developed to mirror my hand calculations and run the rest of the 550 spans.

The morning I finished designing the spiral, I decided to take a break and do nothing. I went outside to the streets

A Person Is a Product of Time, Place, and Circumstances

to see what was going on there. I had no idea what season it was or what was going on in life outside—I had been shut off from life for over 4 months.

Strolling lazily along North Charles Street toward the Harbor Place and looking at some window shops, I entered one small shop and suddenly became dizzy and nauseated; everything started spinning around me.

I was panicked by the familiar symptoms, but this time I knew what it was. I already had a name for it—a brain breakdown. I knew it would not be long before my head went spinning into a black hole resulting in a loss of consciousness.

I needed to save my strength and did not ask anyone for help going to the hospital. I took a risk and chose to drive home immediately, passing the hospital. I drove home, went to bed, and start experiencing vertigo. I was spiraling down a black hole.

Could I come back? I do not know how long I was unconscious, but I reawakened to find myself in bed. But then vertigo returned. With each passing day, these episodes decreased in severity and frequency. I spent 5 days in bed before recovering.

I read somewhere that one executive, after finishing a stressful deadline project, was taking the New York subway home and suddenly got dizzy, nauseated and passed out; he had a nervous breakdown.

THE MORAL OF THE STORY

Everything has a limit, even our minds and brain. When our mind and brain are under tremendous pressure and weight, they can become injured and sick.

The key is to recognize quickly when and why? Nothing happens by accident—there is always a reason why an event or sickness happened, which is another wise law of life applicable here. The last time, when designing the spiral for the Baltimore Subway, I recognized what was about to occur, took quick action, and saved myself.

Even cars are designed with a maximum speed limit. Optimally, cars tend to drive between 55-80 miles per hour (depending on the road); drive above that speed and it become hazardous to drive. An average car designed for everyday needs has a 200–300 horsepower motor, which would burn up if you tried to drive it as a race car at 200 miles per hour.

Even drinking water to hydrogenate yourself has a limit: drink 5–6 glasses of water per day, to keep from becoming dehydrated, but increase it to 8–10 glasses or more, and it can hurt the body, as minerals start being washed out of the body.

SHORT STORY

The Civil Rights Act of 1964 and the Equal Employment Opportunity Commission

A Person Is a Product of Time, Place, and Circumstances

△ △ △

In 1964 Congress passed Civil Rights Act, Public Law 88-352, that forbade discrimination on the bases of sex and race in hiring, promoting, and firing. To enforce the Civil Rights Act of 1964— Equal Employment Opportunity Commission, EEOC, was created in 1965.

The historic Civil Rights Act of 1964 for the first time in the history of the USA granted equal opportunity to women and minorities to enter colleges, and workplaces. But discrimination, prejudice, and abuse of the law persisted for the next 2 or more decades. Even today, women continue earning only 77 cents for every dollar when compared to men. Before 1964, American women had no opportunity to enter the majority of colleges.

As for women engineers, there were even more problems. Only those who were gifted and brilliant were able to graduate from engineering schools, and they were many times brighter than their male counterparts.

Even for them, the reality of getting get hired as an engineer was bleak. They were lucky to work as secretaries in engineering companies. Then, starting in the 1970s, the implementation of Civil Rights Act of 1964 started taking place.

Today younger women have no idea what it was like in the 1970s to enter college, or to get the same job as men. Prejudice, discrimination, gender bias, and even open hostility in the work place were rampant. It was impossible to work, let alone to survive.

My personal experience was not an exception to the rule, it was the rule. Beginning in the 1970s, I was hired as a structural engineer to design bridges—all due to sheer luck. You see, I was a Russian during the Cold War, when fierce technological competition and the battle for world dominance took place between 2 bitter rivals: the USA and the Soviet Union.

American companies saw me as a social experiment to find out from me the difference between Russian and American engineers. Even though I was hired as an engineer, it was just a small step. Ahead of me lay monumental problems, including when I had to prove that I could design a whole bridge all by myself, without any references, templates, or guidance.

Even more dramatic, I was the 1st woman engineer in the company and men engineers became very offended that the top management had hired me. They were sure that from now on, their profession would decline, as if a homemaker (a woman) was going to design a bridge.

Agitated and angered, every day they congregated in small groups not far from my drawing station. Loudly, so that I could hear them clearly, they voiced their disapproval and anger.

A Person Is a Product of Time, Place, and Circumstances

In the 1970s, engineering companies did not have separate offices or cubicles for engineers as there are today. All that was designed to encourage creativity and innovations. The layout of the whole floor in all directions was open, with light and the sun beaming from all directions.

From any location, one could see 360 degrees, across all 4 walls and windows that enveloped the floor. Inside the floor's layout were individual stations (tables and drawing boards) for each engineer, and the stations were exposed to everyone from all directions.

In close proximity to me sat Bill, the main instigator, who was stirring major trouble for me. Later I learned he was a draftsman, a family man, and a breadwinner. He was jealous and could not accept the fact that a woman was an engineer and not him. He barely worked. All day he would entertain visitors—the men engineers who would come to his station to dither and gossip.

He even drafted his own wife as an antagonist. When she telephoned and asked about me, he would turn his rotating chair around, facing me. Then, answering her, he would say loudly: "Oh, she seems to be ok, she's drinking coffee now."

The environment was unfair and hostile, as there was a lot of discontent concerning me. At the same time, on my desk, in front of me, was a field drawing with a prominent red line drawn between point A and point B.

It was my 1st bridge in the air that I would have to design alone, without any guidance or reference whatsoever. I knew very well that if I dared to ask for help or examples, they would use this as a pretense to fire me, justifying their actions with the conclusion that I had no idea how to design a bridge.

That was true; I had no idea, or even a clue as to how to design a bridge. Before coming to the USA, in Africa, I was designing reinforced concrete buildings, in the metric system, using European design methods, and in French. Such a hostile work environment made me fearful. I was suffering and could not concentrate on my problem, my 1st bridge design. My despair continued for several days until an incident occurred.

That day, I was walking across the company's reception area when I crossed paths with Lori. She was from the human resources department. Happy to see me, she hugged me with a bear hug and warmly asked: "How are you doing?"

That was the first time, over the course of several days of male chauvinism that I had met a genuine human being. Bottled up emotions, gushed out. Sobbing and crying uncontrollably, I had a tearful breakdown.

Lori wrapped her hand around my waist and escorted me to her manager, the head of the human resources department, Mr. McGrow. Feeling safe and secure, I poured out to him all the suffering that I had endured over the last several days. It was a turning point.

Immediately, Mr. McGrow called top management to a meeting describing my desperate situation to them. They made a decision to stop the prejudice, hostility, and bullying against me. For the next several days, the top management called the male engineers in small groups to a conference room where they chastised and scolded them over their behavior, emphasizing that times had changed.

The Civil Rights Act of 1964 was here to stay, and they had to stop their prejudice, anger, and hostility toward me, otherwise their own employment would be terminated.

They stopped. Soon, Bill, the major troublemaker, left the company. All the men had stopped talking to him and avoided him. Feeling isolated and ignored, he left.

With the hostile environment gone, I started concentrating on my problem—how to design a bridge all on my own. In the end, a wonder happened and I designed the bridge successfully. It was accepted 100%. The company was so impressed they started looking for another woman engineer.

During this trying time, I met 2 brilliant women engineers; they had graduated as civil engineers, but were working as draftsmen. They introduced me to the Baltimore-Washington Society of Women Engineers.

The majority of its members were women electrical engineers, who worked for Westinghouse in Maryland, which was purchased by the USA government to use for military hardware (in the 1950–1980s).

In this government organization, the women engineers were doing well, since the Civil Rights Act of 1964 had been implemented from its inception.

The women engineers' association was very helpful to me. We met regularly in one of the restaurants in Maryland. We helped each other, and supported and learned from each other.

During our meetings we invited prominent speakers who gave us lectures to enhance our development, gain new information and knowledge, and learn new skills.

As we grew professionally and intellectually, we started raising money for scholarships for young high school girls to enter engineering schools. We gave numerous lectures in high schools to encourage girls to enter engineering schools.

We regularly took different courses to improve our skills and intelligence. Many of us graduated with master's degrees. We had *The Journal of Women Engineers,* today called *The SWE (Society of Women Engineers).* The journal was a great source of information and support to us.

Classic Examples of Opportunity and No Opportunity for Women in College Education in Some Countries in the World

1) In the USA today, 60% of women are graduating with college degrees, while only 40% of American men are.[1] Only in 1964 were American women given an equal opportunity with their male counterparts.

   Although the Civil Rights Act was passed, it took many years for its effects to take hold. The first woman was accepted to Yale University in 1968. Even today American women's salaries are only 77% of American men's.

2) In the Soviet Union, the Revolution of November 1917 gave Soviet women equal opportunity. And after World War II, when 26.6 million Russians were killed, almost all men between age 18 and 50, to replaced the vacant job positions, the Soviet women entered universities in unprecedented numbers.

   And in less than 1 generation, they outperformed men—75% of Russian women graduated from universities, versus 25% of Russian men. Plus, teachers and physicians were over 90% women.

3) Opportunity for women in Iran. In Iran, over 60% of women finished colleges, versus less that 40% of Iranian men.

4) No opportunity exists for women in Saudi Arabia. They are oppressed and are treated as merchandize. Their lives are tragic—they are second-class citizens, must wear veils, and must be escorted everywhere by a man. Only recently in 2011, the 1st university opened for women. But, when they graduate, there will be no jobs for them, as no one is going to hire them.

△ △ △

THE MORAL OF THE STORY

For many centuries, women were discriminated against by men. They endured oppression, abuse, humiliation, and prejudice and were treated as second-class citizens. 1964 was a historic year in the USA—it changed the lives of American women as we know it today.

The Civil Rights Act of 1964 gave women and minorities the equal employment opportunity. This law was signed by President Lyndon Johnson.

The rest, as they say, is history. In less than 2 generations, American women achieved a miracle—they caught up with their men, then—overtook them! Today, 60% of American women are graduating with college degrees versus 40% of American men. As for the Dean's List of honor students? The majority are women.

Today, more women are employed than men; women are savvier in finances and have savings, especially younger generations; they read more and know more about life around them. Endurance, stoicism, perseverance, and high self-esteem have become the new character traits of American women.

---

[1] Please read another story, "How American Women Overtook American Men in Just 2 Generations."

SHORT STORY

How American Women Overtook American Men in Just 2 Generations

Where to Get Information, Knowledge, and Skills

As a young child, when I was scared of something or had problems, I ran to my grandparents, Vasily and Anna, for reassurance, and to solve them. They always had simple answers and solutions.

My question was, when, if ever, would I be as intelligent, and wise as they were? My grandpa reassured me that I would be one day; however, it was going to take some time, and on my part a lot of energy, determination, effort, and hard work.

He expanded my question and also gave his answers. Grandpa put a question to me: "What is the greatest wealth you have?" Then he answered for me: "Information, knowledge, and skills that you have stored in your mind. They are: the schools you went to, courses you took, books you have read, people you have met, places you have travelled and visited.

"This is, acquired information and knowledge that you can take with you anywhere. They are stored in your mind, in your brain storage. If you have a large database, it will help you to find solutions, and save you in all difficult circumstances and challenging events."

Grandpa used the word "storage." Here, I have changed it to "database" to adjust to 21st century terminology. In short: Do you have a problem? Need a solution? Go to your brain database and retrieve the answer. Assume that you have a large database of information, knowledge, and skills when looking for a solution.

How Can One Become Sophisticated, Intelligent, Have Good Manners and Stand Out from the Crowd?

I was in the 3rd grade when my best friend Galina let me borrow her book for a few days. It was Mark Twain's *Adventures of Tom Sawyer and Huckleberry Finn*. I started reading it and read it through the night. From that time, I was hooked on books and became an avid reader and dreamer.

By the time I graduated from university, I had read scores of classics from all over the world.[1] I had a personal collection and library by my favorite writers. I loved story telling. In novels, I could be anything I wanted to be, including my heroes. I adopted their character traits, attitudes, behavior, and manners. I became one of them. Sophisticated, intelligent, and knowledgeable. The way I talked, walked, and dressed made every teenager want to have me as her friend.

I had a lot of energy and was very curious and fascinated with the world and people around me. Every person I met—regardless of their education, age or status—they became my instant mentors.

I looked up to new people, listened, and absorbed new information and skills from them. I never became jealous of anyone who was better off, prettier, or more educated than I was. I did not have such petty emotions.

Intelligence Is Learned Not Inherited

When growing up in Odessa on the Black Sea, my best friends were the most sophisticated girls in my city; they were honor student, or grade "A" students: intelligent, passionate book readers, and dreamers.

We would help each other with all our issues and problems. If one of us was lagging in any subject, immediately the others, who knew that subject better, became her tutor so no one was left behind.

We never missed any popular movies. We regularly went to the opera, theatre, drama plays, and the circus. We also visited the philharmonic and were regular listeners of concerts of classical music. Even though I was not very passionate about it, I tagged along with my friends who were enthusiastic about classical music.

We put our energy into being "A" students in every subject and grade. We spent summer vacations working summer jobs, and on weekends we sunbathed on the beach, talked and discussed books and plays, and made observations about life and people.

Evenings were magic. We went dancing anywhere where popular music was playing and the crowd had gathered. Sleepovers were typical. Intoxicated by life adventures, we talked and dreamed late into the nights.

Then came my time in engineering school. The school was very difficult; honestly, it was hell. Many years later, I continued having nightmares that I did not graduate. At that time, my major priority and dream in life was to graduate from university with a civil engineering degree. And it was questionable whether that would happen. Some of my best friends, straight "A" students, did not graduate. Almost all exams were oral, and professors did not care whether you had A's in other subjects. If you were not up to the challenge in his subject, you got an F and failed.

Russian professors were former scientists. They received a professorship for life, and had supreme power at the university, and students were intimidated by them, and avoided them.

In 1917, after the November Revolution in the USSR, women received equal opportunity. That was why in my generation, 75% of Russian women received bachelor degrees versus 25% of Russian men. Russian women made up 50% were of university graduate engineers and were over 90% of teacher and physician graduates. Engineering was and is today the most prestigious profession in the world, except in the USA.

Discrimination, Prejudice, Hostility, and Abuse

The historic Civil Right Act of 1964 for the first time in the history of the USA allowed American women and minorities to enter colleges and workplaces free from prejudice.[2]

But discrimination, prejudice, hostility, and abuse of the law was rampant and continued for the next 2 or more decades. Even today, women continue earning only 77 cents for every dollar, compared to men. Before 1964, American women had little opportunity to enter the majority of colleges and complete on par with men.

As for women engineers, there were even more problems. Only those who were gifted and brilliant were able to graduate from engineering schools; they were many times brighter than their male counterparts. Even for them, the prospects of getting hired as an engineer were bleak. Then, starting in the mid-1970s, little by little, change started taking place with equal opportunity.

How American Women Overtook Men in Just 2 Generations

Feeling sorry for men (I studied and worked almost all my life with men), and felling sorry especially for young men (I have 2 sons and 2 grandsons), very often I asked them: "Do you know that today, 60% of American women have graduated with a bachelor's degree versus 40% of American men? Even more, on every university's Dean's List, the majority are women."

The majority of men have no clue, are very surprised and asking: "Why? What are the reasons?" Indeed, how did such a phenomenon happen in just 2 generations? Nothing happened by an accident, there were reasons for this, as below.

Reason #1

The historic Civil Rights Act of 1964 gave American women equal footing with men. Before 1964, the majority of American colleges did not accept women. Now women were given fair consideration.

The rest was up to them: to fail, survive, or prosper. American women faced monumental problems though: to catch up with men, they had to develop personal abilities as soon as possible, combat and overcome prejudice and ignorance, survive in hostile work and educational environments, and at the same time continue to carry on their primary duties of being mothers, housekeepers, and wives.

Women's destinies were in their own hands and under their control. Until then, only men had all the opportunities—they were in charge of the all professions for hundreds of years.

Women were submissive and were treated as second-class citizens; they played mostly the roles of mothers, wives, and housewives.

Reason #2

Unsure of themselves, looking for support and guidance, women started many organizations, clubs, and associations. There they obtained information, motivation, and support. Looking for women's clubs and associations to join? Go on the internet; there you can find hundreds of them.

Reason #3

After women became college students en masse, they put all their energy and focus on their studies, took nothing for granted, and studied hard. The environment was hostile and unfavorable.

To receive the same grades or occupy the same position as a man did, a woman had to be more intelligent and sophisticated, and have more information and knowledge than her male counterpart. Only then would she be appraised as "She is o k." But, if her knowledge and information was on the same level as a man's, she had no chance: "She knows nothing."

In just in 2 generations, American women have made spectacular progress. They not only caught up with their male counterparts in numbers of university graduates, they surpassed them. Today, 60% of American women are university graduates versus 40% of men.

Just ask men if they knew these statistics. Chances are they do not; they are very much detached from the world around them.

Reason #4

Women became prolific book readers. The majority of books are bought and read by women. Women read magazines and many journals from their clubs and associations, they attend numerous lectures and conferences, and they are the major participants on PBS (Public Broadcast Services).

Reason #5

Women became financially independent. Financial gurus like Suze Orman are celebrated example. From Suze Orman, they learned how to save, how to make rational financial decisions, and manage their finances.

That is why women bought and read her books and listened to all her shows. They are the major attendees at her talks and other PBS presentations. Just watch a few episodes of the *People's Court* TV show.

Judges on those types of shows always point out that the plaintiffs, the lenders of the money, are often women. The defendants, the debtors, are often men.

Very often I have asked men: do you know Suze Orman? No, is a typical answer. The name is not familiar to them, and they have never heard of her. Only a few men have: "Oh, you are probably talking about the lady that my girlfriend is watching?"

Reason #6

Women are flexible; they can work in many different types of work and industries. That is because they have acquired many skills that are transferable from one industry to another.

In addition, they carried out extra responsibilities that required different sets of skills, including being mothers, wives, and housekeepers. How were women able to make it? You see women's engagement in the above activities, reasons #1–#5, accumulated a huge storage of needed information, knowledge, and skills in their brain database.

Got a new job? Faced with new challenges? No problem—retrieve the answers and solutions from your huge brain storage.

Reason #7

African American women's contribution to society should not be overlooked and ignored. It should be saluted with gratitude. African American women are subjected to racial discrimination in addition to gender bias and prejudice.

But they are the backbone of their families. Where 72% of new babies are born out of wedlock, and who is looking after and raising these children?

Grandmothers. African American women of all ages and skills have been compelled to persevere under the dual evils of race and gender bias, and discrimination.

THE MORAL OF THE STORY

Information is: knowledge, power, and wealth. Your success and survival all depend on the amount of information, knowledge, and skills you have stored in your brain's database! You can increase this storage through: books you read; schools you attend; classes you take; people you meet; mentors you have had; associations and clubs you join; places you visit, and travel to and from.

The probability of solving all your problems and saving your life from unpredictable circumstances and dramatic events all depend on the volume of information stored in your brain's database.

That probability is raised according to the volume of the database you have in your brain (that is why a child who has not yet had enough time to develop a large volume of information and knowledge in his database cannot solve problems that adults can).

Information is: knowledge, power, and wealth. Intelligence is learned, not inherited. Education is how American women in just 2 generations caught up with men and left them behind! Today 60% of American women are graduating from colleges versus 40% of American men.

---

[1] Some classic books I have read were by Mark Twain, Charles Dickens, Victor Hugo, Jules Verne, Sir Arthur Conan Doyle, Alexandre Dumas, Jack London, Jane Austen, William Shakespeare, Ernest Hemingway, Lord George Byron, Bernard Shaw, Emile Zola, Stendhal, Guy de Maupassant, George Sand (a female French writer), Gustave Flaubert, Homer, Balzac, Goethe, Allan Poe, Oscar Wilde, Emily Dickinson, Emily Bronte, Erich Maria Remarque (my favorite), and many, many more...

Some books (I do not remember the authors' names): Don Quixote, Arabian Nights, Uncle Tom's Cabin, White Slave, Gulliver's Travels, Aladdin and the Magic Lamp, Amok, the Forsyte Saga, Upstairs Downstairs, etc.

Of course there were also books by many Russian writers' and poets: Leo Tolstoy, Fyodor Dostoyevsky, Nikolai Gogol, Anton Chekhov, Alexander Pushkin, Nikolai Lermontov, etc.

My favor American writer was Theodor Dreiser. I had a collection of all his books in hardcover: Sister Carrie, An American Tragedy, The Financier, The Titan, The Stoic, The Genius, etc.

[2] Please read another story: "Historic Equal Employment Opportunity (EEO) Act of 1964."

SHORT STORY

The Great Event of the 20th Century that Changed the World: Vladimir Ilyich Lenin and the Russian Revolution of November 6–7, 1917

A Person Is a Product of Time, Place, and Circumstances

△ △ △

The greatest event of the 20th century was the Russian Revolution of November 6–7, 1917. It changed the world.

The architect of the Russian Revolution was Vladimir Ilyich Lenin. Lenin was the most important person of the 20th century; he changed the world into 2 systems: capitalism and socialism.

Socialism and the Russian Revolution's many decrees reverberated across the world and changed the lives of every person on this planet as we know it today: equal opportunity for all; women were equal to men in voting, in education, and in work; 4-month maternity leaves and free child care for women, as well as the rights to have abortions; free health care; free education for all citizens; labor laws (8-hour workday), and minimum wages; prohibition of child labor; no dangerous working conditions; sick leaves; 2–4 weeks of vacation time; pensions and benefits; and many more.

Who was Vladimir Ilyich Ulyanov, whose pseudonym was Lenin? Why do the Russians worship him, and why does the world admires his genius?

How did he start the greatest event of the 20th century—the Russian Revolution of November 1917 that overthrew the Russian tsar's (emperor's) regime and transformed backward Russia into the USSR (the Union of Soviet Socialist Republics or, the Soviet Union), where workers and peasants became in charge of their country? Why and how did he change the world?

Vladimir Ulyanov, which was his family name, was born into a privileged family on April 22, 1870, in Simbirsk on the Volga River, a town that today is known as Ulyanovsk.[1] His father, Ilya Nikolayevich Ulyanov, was a mathematics and physics teacher who had risen into the ranks of the Russian nobility as a provincial director of elementary education. His mother, Maria, was also a teacher.

His parents instilled in their children a desire to learn and the commitment to improve the lives of ordinary Russians.

Vladimir lived a privileged life, which was typical of other children of the Russian upper class. He attended a gymnasium (high school) for Russian nobility; he was a serious honor student, finished high school with a gold medal, and was proficient in Latin and Greek.

During Vladimir's high school years, he never thought or dreamed of being a revolutionary or changing the world, until destiny intervened and ambushed his young mind with a tragic event that changed his life forever. As a result of this event, he transformed the lives of Russians and the world.

When Vladimir was 16 years old, his father died. Then 1 year later, on May 8, 1887, just a few weeks before his graduation from high school, his older brother Aleksandr was executed by hanging at Shlisselburg in the middle of the fortress yard with 4 other student conspirators who were caught trying to assassinate Tsar Alexander III of Russia.

Shocked and traumatized from the dramatic execution of his brother, whom he idolized, this tragic event produced unanswered questions in Vladimir's young mind: "Why did my brother, a bright student, who had everything in his life and whose successful life was still all ahead of him, choose to terminate it at the age of 21 for a cause to assassinate the Tsar?"

His brother Aleksandr, after leaving the college of Smolensk with honors in 1883, entered St. Petersburg University to study the natural sciences.

While at the university, he joined many student groups whose objectives were to make Russia a democratic, industrial, and developed country just like Europe.

At that time, Russia was ruled by the emperors, known as tsars, whose rule was hereditary. The last emperors were the Romanovs, and their family ruled Russia for 300 years. Young students saw the tsars as problems; they were holding Russia back.

Aleksandr Ulyanov and his comrades began plotting an assassination attempt on Tsar Alexander III. That was not the 1st attempt to assassinate a Russian tsar.

For generations before this, students from noble Russian families continuously plotted to assassinate many Russian tsars. Sometimes they were successful and killed or wounded some tsars. Even though they were the sons and daughters of the wealthiest families from the richest and largest empire on Earth, they did not care about their personal wealth or their prosperous lives.

What they cared about was a mighty Russia, and they were ready to give up their young lives to fight for Russia's liberation from the tsar's tyranny and repression of the ordinary Russian people. They wanted to see a progressive and democratic Russia.

On March 1, 1887, which marked the 6th anniversary of the assassination of Tsar Alexander II, Aleksandr Ulyanov and his conspirators were plotting to assassinate his son, the current emperor of Russia, Tsar Alexander III.

But they were arrested in St. Petersburg on its main street, Nevsky Prospect.[2] Aleksandr Ulyanov was the chemist preparing the bombs, and he gave a political speech during the court proceedings.

Aleksandr's mother, Maria, visited him in prison and begged him to ask for the tsar's clemency, but he refused. However, some of his conspirators petitioned the tsar and their death sentences were commuted.

On May 8, 1887, Aleksandr Ulyanov and 4 of his coconspirators were executed by hanging in a fortress

A Person Is a Product of Time, Place, and Circumstances

or prison located on an island known as Oreshek in Shlisselburg, near St. Petersburg. Today a plaque to Aleksandr Ulyanov can be found on the spot in the courtyard where he was hanged.

After his brother's execution in 1887, Vladimir entered Kazan University but soon was expelled for his demonstration activities. He was permitted to retire to a family estate and obtained a law degree as an outside student in 1890.

While living on his family estate, he had access to his family's extensive private library. To broaden his knowledge about his executed brother's cause, he immersed himself in reading many books and was intoxicated by the Marxism of Karl Marx and Friedrich Engels.

There, after 3 years, he found the answer and emerged with a real solution to the revolutionary struggle. "We are not going to take my brother Aleksandr's path," Vladimir's well-known solution was. "To assassinate a Tsar is not the solution. An assassinated Tsar is always replaced by another Tsar next in the dynastic line, and he may be even more despotic and a worse tyrant. We are going to change the regime." In 1890 Vladimir obtained a law degree with honors from the University of St. Petersburg.

One thing was obvious—in those years of searching for the answer, Vladimir himself became a revolutionary and had only one mission in life.

Only a revolution could overthrow the tsar's regime and put his mighty Russia on the path of industrial development and freedom. From then on, he began using "we," which meant him and his revolutionary comrades.

To join the revolutionary movement in 1893, he moved to St. Petersburg, the Russian capital at that time, and took an active role in the student movements. Russian universities were cradles for student revolutionary movements, and the tsar's police had a prominent footing on all campuses to disrupt, weed out, and catch anti tsar students.

Soon it happened to Vladimir. In December 1897, he was arrested, jailed for 1 year, and then sent to a remote area of Siberia for 3 years.

In 1898 he married Nadezhda Krupskaya, a fellow Marxist; she was a teacher, and also came from a noble Russian family. After he escaped from Siberia in 1900, he moved to Europe where he spent the next 17 years plotting the Russian revolution and lived on the financial support his mother, Maria, provided.

Switzerland was an exile center for Russian revolutionaries. They all came from the Russian upper class and did not need to work to earn a living. Instead, they spent their time learning, discussing, writing, and organizing the revolution for the Russian workers and peasants who had no time and opportunity to study, learn, and become intellectuals.

"We will do the revolution for them" was the established answer of the Lenin and Russian revolutionaries. Now Lenin (he took his pseudonym) became a major leader. He spoke 7 languages, wrote many papers in many languages, and gave impassionate speeches.

His writings and forceful speeches concentrated on the proletariat movement and on the intellectuals to promote his revolution. Lenin and others founded a newspaper in Munich, *Iskra* (*Spark*), to promote their ideas and unify all Marxists.

In the last decade of the 19th century, Russia underwent a rapid growth of industry, and cities populated by the proletariat (burgeoning industrial workers) were growing rapidly. Intellectuals were the highly educated, philosophers from the upper class who were developing theories for the revolutionary movement and provided the guidance and implementation. In 1902 Lenin expressed those ideas in his seminal book *What Is to Be Done?*

Bloody Sunday, 1905

Bloody Sunday on January 22, 1905, in St. Petersburg, Russia, was the precursor for the November 1917 Revolution.[3] Before Bloody Sunday, Russian workers retained the conservative values of Orthodoxy, and to them God had sent the Tsar to help them.

They had a deep faith in the autocracy and an indifference to political life. During January there were many strikes in over 300 factories, and 150,000 workers went on strike protesting the firing of their coworkers and the inhumane conditions in their factories.

A Russian priest, Father Gapon, who was concerned about the conditions in the factories for workers, drafted himself a petition calling for improved working conditions, fair wages, and a reduction of the working day to 8 hours.

This petition was intended to bring the workers' grievances to the tsar's administration or to the tsar himself when he appeared outside of his Winter Palace. Father Gapon gave this petition to the Winter Palace days before the march.

On Sunday, striking workers and their families began gathering in 6 points in St Petersburg preparing to march, and by 2:00 p.m. all began to converge in front of the Winter Palace, the tsar's residence. They carried religious icons and banners and portraits of the Tsar, and sang "God Save the Tsar." Women, children, and the elderly marched in front of the demonstrations, showing their peaceful intentions.

No Bolsheviks (the Majority), Mensheviks (the Minority), or Social Democrats—the political groups at that time—were involved in this demonstration. There were no political demands in the workers' petition and to some of them, Father Gapon was "a police representative" of the tsar.

The tsar left his Winter Palace for his retreat, Tsarskoye Selo, but ordered demonstrators to be contained.

A Person Is a Product of Time, Place, and Circumstances

Permanent imperial guard units and Cossacks, plus infantry regiments brought in by rail in the early morning, encircled the Winter Palace.

In total, the tsar's troops numbered about 10,000 strong, ready and waiting to face the marchers while 2,300 more guards were held in reserve.

The 1st shooting at peaceful marchers occurred between 10:00 and 11:00 a.m. and continued until 2:00 p.m. as new groups of marchers, unaware of the violence and killings, reached their planned Winter Palace destination.

The number of those killed and wounded is uncertain. The tsar's officials recorded 96 dead and 333 injured; antigovernment sources claimed 4,000 deaths, with moderate estimates around 1,000 dead and wounded. Father Gapon quickly left Russia, and after he revealed to his friend that he was also a secret police agent, he was assassinated.

Bloody Sunday reverberated across the country, revolts flared up and ignited strikes in numerous cities, and 3 million workers went on strike.

The tsar again resorted to brutal force, and by the end of 1905, he had hanged and shot 15,000 workers and peasants, injured 20,000, and exiled 45,000.

The major outcome of Bloody Sunday and the tsar's violence and brutality was a 180 degrees change in the attitudes of the workers and peasants.

From then on, the tsar was no longer "Sent by God to protect and take care of the people." Instead, now the tsar was an enemy, an autocratic despot killing and exploiting his poor people. Lenin and the Bolsheviks capitalized on this new attitude.

The Time Was Ripe for the Revolution. Lenin Returned to St. Petersburg on April 16, 1917, from Switzerland

Tsar Nicholas II forced 11 million Russian peasants to fight against the Germans in the unpopular World War I, 1914–1918; many were brutally killed and injured. In February 1917 a mass demonstration of women factory workers protested their harsh working conditions.

When the tsar called out the army to quash the protestors, the women convinced the soldiers to take their side, and the tsar was abdicated. A provisional government consisting of capitalists, bankers, and lawyers was formed, and they continued with the war.

The time was ripe for a revolution.

Lenin returned to St. Petersburg on April 16, 1917, from Switzerland to direct the boiling revolution. He published his "April Theses" in the Bolshevik newspaper *Pravda (Truth)* and joined the Bolshevik Party to overthrow the provisional government and establish a government for the proletariat.

The Russian Revolution of November 6–7, 1917, that Changed the World

In October 1917 Lenin convinced the Bolshevik Party to seize the moment and act quickly. The Red Guards and other revolutionary groups moved on the night of November 6–7 and seized the telegraph, post offices, railroad stations, electric works, and state banks.

Once the shot from the battleship *Aurora* was fired, signaling the beginning of the revolution, thousands of revolutionaries stormed the Winter Palace. The Winter Palace fell, and on that news, the proletariats (workers, soldiers, and peasants) rose, and the revolution triumphed.

Vladimir Lenin, the leader of the revolution, formed the Soviet government and passed the Decrees on Peace and Land. Private land was distributed to peasants. Other decrees followed: all private banks were confiscated and nationalized; church properties and bank accounts were seized; control of factories was given to the new Soviet government; and an 8-hour working day was established with higher wages.

The 1917 Russian Revolution gave equal rights and opportunity to all. Russian women received equal rights to vote, and millions entered universities and technical schools.

As for Muslim women, who were living in some of the 15 smaller Soviet republics, it was a joyous and exciting time. The day equal rights were announced, many Muslim women tore off their veils and threw them away.

The result of the November revolution was a bitter 4-year Civil War which started between the White Army (imperial counter-revolutionaries of Tsar Nicholas II) and the new pro-revolutionary Red Army (Bolsheviks) from 1918–1922. The Red Army eventually defeated the White Army.

Lenin Pulled Russia out of World War I

The Russian Revolution of November 1917 had a major impact on World War I, WWI, 1914–1918, between Europe, Britain, the Russian Empire, and Germany.

The majority of the fighting was between the Russians and the Germans. Then, the Russian Revolution of 1917 under the leader of the Bolshevik party, Vladimir Lenin, overthrew the tsar's regime, and workers and peasants took charge of their own country.

Vladimir Lenin saw impossible difficulties for the new Socialist state and Red Army to fight 3 wars on 3 fronts: World War I, the Revolution, and the Civil War. Lenin postulated that the capitalists—rich manufacturers, industrialists, and bankers—started the war to make money at the expense of the working class who suffered the most. For this reason, by all means, he must pull Russia out of World War I.

He did. Lenin asked Germany to end the war and sign a peace treaty with Russia. Germany was in a much better situation than socialist Russia and agreed to stop the war with the Russians, provided that in return Russia gave them some Russian territory.

Specifically, Germany wanted to have access to the Baltic Sea (Estonia, Latvia, and Lithuania) and the Western Ukraine, including the city of Lvov (next to Poland). Lenin had no other alternative and agreed. In November 1918 the Bolshevik government signed the Brest-Litovsk Treaty with Germany, pulled out of the war, and accepted those territorial losses.

The casualties of World War I were as follows: the Imperial Russian Empire lost 3.4 million; Germany lost 2.8 million; Britain lost 1.0 million; and the USA lost 117,000.

Lenin Formally Established the Union of Soviet Socialist Republics (the USSR, or the Soviet Union), 1922

Lenin fulfilled the nation's demand for: "Peace, bread and land." In 1918 the ruling Bolshevik Party was renamed the All-Russian Communist Party and began consolidating its power and took control of the smaller 15 states bordering Russia.

In 1922 Lenin formally established the Soviet Union (Union of Soviet Socialist Republics, or USSR), and changed the world into 2 systems—capitalism and socialism—and the world economy into 2 economies—a free capitalist market economy and a centrally planned socialist economy.

2 Serious Assassination Attempts on Lenin and His Death

Once Russia pulled out of World War I, Germany moved its army from the Eastern Front to the Western Front to quash Britain and Europe. The major fight had been between the Russians and the Germans, and the British wanted the Russians back in the war. Lenin was their obstacle, so they sent their agents to assassinate him.

In the 2nd assassination attempt on August 30, 1918, Fayer Kaplan fired 3 shots and seriously wounded Lenin. She refused to disclose whose agent she was, and the next day she herself was shot.

Lenin could not recover from the assassination attempts, had 3 strokes, and died on January 24, 1924; he was 54 years old. Joseph Stalin then became the leader of the USSR.

After Lenin's death, the Soviet government received hundreds of thousands of requests from people all over the world asking them to preserve Lenin's body, and many pathologists and embalmers came to Moscow to offer their knowledge and information about the embalming process.

Lenin's body was embalmed and then put into a newly built granite structure, Lenin's Mausoleum, situated next to the Kremlin in Red Square. Millions of visitors,

Russians and foreigners, still come to Lenin's Mausoleum to see him.

Summary

The greatest 20th-century event—the Russian Revolution of November 6–7, 1917 happened because of one great man: Vladimir Ilyich Lenin (birth name Ulyanov).

How was this one man, who believed he had a greater purpose in life, which elevated him above his personal selfishness to a much higher level, able to transform backward imperial Russia into an industrial country and give workers and peasants a decent quality of life, as well as dignity and honor?

What were the events and circumstances responsible for Vladimir Ulyanov's sudden transformation from a 17-year-old youth into a great thinker and revolutionary who desired to change the world? Several *Laws of life from Wisdom and Experience* in the trilogy were at work, as seen below.

Law of Life in book 3 in this trilogy: it is from the short story "Nothing Happens by Accident, There Is Always a Reason for it."

Vladimir was lucky; he lived a privileged life. At age 17 he was about to graduate from gymnasium (high school) in a few weeks, and at that time was not dreaming about becoming a revolutionary or changing the world. He was a hardworking student, an honors student, fluent in Latin and Greek, and graduated with a gold medal.

Then his family received the tragic news that his older brother Aleksandr, a student at St. Petersburg University, whom he idolized, was executed by hanging after his attempt to assassinate the Tsar of Russia, Alexander III.

Stunned, shaken, puzzled, and confused, on that day, Vladimir grew up quickly from a teenager into an adult, continuously searching for an answer to the question, "Why did my older brother, whose whole life was still ahead of him, choose to sacrifice his young life at the age of 21 in an attempt to assassinate the Tsar?"

In autumn, he entered university and joined student revolutionary organizations to learn more about his brother's cause. Soon he was arrested and sent into exile to his family estate.

There for 3 years, he immersed himself in reading books, searching for an answer. He found the answer and moved back to St. Petersburg to again join the student revolutionary organizations.

Law of Life in this book: it is from the short story "A Person Is a Product of Time, Place, and Circumstances."

Vladimir Lenin was a product of time, place, and circumstances.

Time: in 1861, Russian serfs on private estates were emancipated and became industrial workers working in factories. At the end of the 19th century, Russian workers and peasants were discontented with their hard lives.

In 1905 Bloody Sunday drastically changed their attitudes from being submissive to their tsar—"The God appointed the Tsar to look after us"—to thinking the tsar was an enemy and a despot.

Place: Russia was ruled by tsars who were holding Russia back from industrial development and democracy, which was occurring in Europe.

Circumstances: 17-year-old Vladimir Ulyanov experienced tragic circumstances. His older brother, 21-year-old Aleksandr, attempted to assassinate the tsar and was executed. Traumatized and puzzled why his brother gave his life, Vladimir set in motion his quest to find the answer.

For the next 3 years, he read hundreds of books and newspapers, became an intellectual, and found the answer.

Law of Life in book 1 in this trilogy: it is from the short story "What Is Quality of Life? Or, a Conversation Between an Eagle and Snake."

The moral of the story is this: Who do you want to be—a snake that lives 300 years and spends all its existence inside a deep hole scared of any noise, or an eagle who lives 80 years and is free to fly everywhere to see cities, children, people, cars, animals, rivers, oceans, mountains, and changes in the weather and seasons?

It teaches us the importance of quality, not quantity, of life. It is not how long a person has lived, but how much he saw, experienced, accomplished, and contributed to society.

Law of Life in book 1 in this trilogy: it is from the short story "What Is Happiness? What Were the Happiest Years in Your Life?"

It is not money and wealth. Even though wealth can improve the quality of one's life, the majority of rich people are unhappy.

Happiness is a higher hierarchy of human development. It is to have a purpose to live for something, to do something important for a common good so that later, before you die, you can look back and be proud you did not live a selfish life, made a contribution to others, and left monuments after yourself.

Vladimir Ilyich Lenin changed the regime and the world—from the tsar's imperial regime into a socialist regime where the working class, for the first time in Russian history, was now in charge of a government and all the citizens were treated equally.

The new Soviet Union regime became socialist. The world was changed into 2 systems: capitalism and socialism.

The Soviet Union as a new country blossomed and became strong and proud. During World War II (1941–1945),

Hitler took over all of Europe in just 3 months—but not the Soviet Union. Stoically, Russians fought Hitler on their own land for 3 years and defeated the Germans in the bloodiest battles of Moscow, Stalingrad, and Berlin.

It was a huge sacrifice because of the 26.6 million Russians who were killed, almost all men between the ages of 18 to 50, and the country was ruined. The Soviet Union won World War II and saved the world and civilization from Nazi Fascism. The USSR then became a world superpower.

Let's repeat it again.

△ △ △

THE MORAL OF THE STORY

The greatest event of the 20th century was the Russian Revolution of November 6–7, 1917, when the 700-year-old Imperial Russian Empire became a new socialist country, the Soviet Union or the USSR, where workers and peasants were put in charge.

The Russian Revolution changed the world into 2 systems: capitalism and socialism. After World War II, the USA, Western Europe, Japan, and Canada were capitalists.

The rest of the world—the Soviet Union, China, India, Africa, Asia, South America, Cuba, and Eastern Europe—were socialists.

The Russian Revolution started and succeeded only due to one great man—Vladimir Ilyich Lenin (birth name Ulyanov). This man believed he had a greater purpose in life, which elevated him above his personal selfishness to a much higher level to transform his backward imperial Russia into an industrial country and give workers and peasants a decent quality of life, as well as dignity and self-respect.

Human history is filled with revolutions, and there have been over 700 revolutions, but only 2 succeeded. One was the Russian Revolution of November 6–7, 1917; the other was the Chinese Revolution in 1949.

History shows again how the power of one man, Vladimir Ilyich Lenin, has changed Russia and the world into 2 systems: capitalism and socialism.

Socialism and the Russian Revolution's many decrees reverberated across the world and

A Person Is a Product of Time, Place, and Circumstances

changed the lives of every person on this planet as we know it today: equal opportunity for all; women were equal to men in voting, in education, and in work; 4-month maternity leave and free child care for women, as well as rights to have abortions; free health care and free education for all citizens; labor laws (8-hour workday) and minimum wages; prohibition of child labor; no dangerous working conditions; sick leave; 2-4 weeks of vacation time; pensions and benefits, and many more.

---

[1] .biography.com/people/vladimir-lenin-9379007
.historyleningsite.co.uk/lockhart_plot.htm
[2] en.wikipedia.org/wiki/Aleksandr_Ulyanov
[3] .funfront.net/hist/russia/revo1905.htm
en.wikipedia.org/wiki/Bloody_Sunday (1905)
.wikipedia.org/wiki/Treaty_of_Brest-Litovsk

SHORT STORY #9

Technological Invention That Shocked the World in the 20th Century. Or, the Russians Launched Sputnik on October 4, 1957

A Person Is a Product of Time, Place, and Circumstances

△ △ △

On October 4, 1957, history was made. The Soviet Union launched Sputnik, the world's first artificial satellite, which orbited the earth and beeped signals across the world.

The world was shocked, fascinated, and astonished—it had not expected this technological progress for many generations.

The Sputnik ("Companion" in English) was silver in color, weighed 184 pounds, and was orbiting the earth every 90 minutes at a speed of 18,000 miles per hour, while broadcasting signals back to Earth.

There was a panic in the Vatican; it protested that the sky and heavens belonged to God, not to Sputnik.

Sputnik's impact on the world and on the USA was colossal, impressive, and unprecedented; it changed the world forever and shaped life as we know it today. It meant that the same rockets that launched the Sputnik into space could send a nuclear warhead across the globe in minutes. The Russians were capable of launching ballistic missiles aimed anywhere in the world.

Even today, those people who in 1957 were old enough to remember recall it as if it happened just yesterday, and where they were and what they were doing when the news of Sputnik hit them.

They were watching the silver Sputnik with the naked eye early in the morning and late in the evening. Sputnik was moving in the sky, orbiting the earth and sending back signals—*"Beep, Beep, Beep"*—announcing its prominent presence. They witnessed history in the making, right before their very own eyes.

Shortly after Sputnik, on November 3, 1957 the Russians this time sent a dog into space, a stray dog, Siberian husky named Laika. Unfortunately, she did not survive reentry into the earth's atmosphere.

More Russian dogs, Belka and Strelka, flew into space on August 19, 1960. They orbited the earth and returned back alive. Then on February 22, 1966, 2 Russian dogs, Veterok and Ugolyok, orbited earth for 22 days, a record-breaking time, and made it back to earth alive.

On April 12, 1961, history was made yet again. Yuri Gagarin[1] boarded Vostok-1 at the Baikonur Cosmodrome and blasted into outer space, where no man had been before.

Yuri Gagarin (1934–1968) was a Russian-Soviet cosmonaut, pilot, and the 1st human to break the barrier of gravity when taking his dangerous voyage into space.

After orbiting the earth for 108 minutes at the top speed of 28,260 km per hour (17,600 miles per hour), Vostok-1 reentered the earth's atmosphere.

A Person Is a Product of Time, Place, and Circumstances

The young pilot parachuted back to earth, and Yuri Gagarin became the 1st man in space. After returning back to earth, Yuri went on a world tour of goodwill. The world loved and admired Yuri Gagarin; he always beamed like the sun. Yuri received over 1 million letters from his fans from all over the world; 50 years later, the majority of the people on this planet still know who Yuri Gagarin was.

That was the mighty period of the Soviet Union. Behind Sputnik's triumph and Yuri Gagarin as the 1st man in space stood the rocket genius Sergei Korolev, the chief rocket engineer and founder of the Soviet space program.

His genius created and pioneered many revolutionary technologies for the 1st time in history, such as: intercontinental missiles; satellites; Sputnik; dogs in space; men in space; human crews in space; directed walk in space; communication satellites; spacecraft towards the moon, Venus, and Mars.

Before Sputnik, Americans were complacent with everyday life. After World War II a new class, the middle class or, the consumers, was born and was growing. Interstate highways were being built along with suburbs. Ownership of single homes, private cars, and color TVs were the object of every American's desire.

Sputnik caught the world's attention and triggered new technological, scientific, military, and political developments. The American public reacted to the Sputnik launch with the same intensity as in previous crises, like the bombing of Pearl Harbor by the Japanese and the death of President Franklin D. Roosevelt.

Sputnik brought a sudden crisis of confidence and self-esteem, a crisis in technology, military, education, politics, and attitudes. A new world order had begun, and what would the USA do about it?

President Dwight Eisenhower's attitude was to underscore the importance of the Sputnik launch and try to downplay this technological success. This did not resonate with the American people. In Sputnik, they saw American weakness and a science gap, that engineering talents were being wasted on frivolous consumption and comfort, fear the USA military had fallen behind, and the role the Eisenhower-Nixon administration played in it.

The Sputnik crisis poured additional funds into the nascent space program to catch up. Until now, the USA had tested several rockets and missiles but all ended in failure. In a hurry, the USA Defense Department approved a USA satellite project, and Eisenhower put Wernher von Braun in charge,[2] a brilliant German rocket engineer and space architect, to speed up the USA's satellite program. In the end, on January 31, 1958, the USA launched its first satellite Explorer, and the space and arms race with the Soviet Union intensified.

The Sputnik crisis forced the USA government to hurriedly launch several initiatives. Education was remapped, pouring a huge amount of funds into science and engineering across all levels of education and initiating a new generation of engineers; military research was assembled; high level DOD (Department of Defense) was established; NASA (National Aeronautics and Space Act) was created; funds for NSF (National Science Foundation) were quadrupled. Thus the space and arms races between the USA and the Soviet Union had begun in earnest.

△ △ △

THE MORAL OF THE STORY

On October 4, 1957 the technological invention that shocked the world in the 20th century was—the Soviet Sputnik.

A crisis always challenges the people's complacency, preparedness, and self-confidence. It always brings new changes, produces new attitudes, and propels people to much higher levels of technological development, as was the case of Sputnik.

Space programs and arms races between the USA and the Soviet Union started and produced the greatest inventions and innovations in human history. Thousands of them spilled over into the civilian sector and improved the quality of everyday lives of people all over the world. The impact of the Sputnik is seen even today, as it produced today's information technology.

---

[1] http://en.wikipedia.org/wiki/Yuri_Gagarin
http://history1900s.about.com/od/1960s/a/yurigagarin.htm
http://history.nasa.gov/sputnik/
Sergei Korolev: "The rocket genius behind Yuri Gagarin," Robin McKie, the Observer, Saturday 12 March 2011.

[2] "Sputnik's Impact on America" by Paul Dickson, posted 11.06.07, NOVA
http://en.wikipedia.org/wiki/Sputnik_1
www.history.com/this-day-in-history/von-braun-moves-to-nasa
https://history.state.gov/milestones/1953-1960/sputnik

SHORT STORY

Why Was the Soviet Union Fighting in Afghanistan Before the USA?

△ △ △

Between December 24, 1979 to February 15, 1988, why was the Soviet Union fighting a 9 year old war against the Mujahedeen and Osama bin Laden in Afghanistan, before the USA?

The center stage for the Afghanistan conflict was set up as follows: from the 1920s and then later from 1950–1992, the Soviet Union promoted a socialist regime that was for the emancipation of Afghan women, the education of girls, and the abolishment of polygamy.

Then in 1979, seeing that the socialist regime in Afghanistan was weakening, the Soviet Union's 40th Army invaded Afghanistan and for the next 9 years fought the Mujahedeen and Osama Bin Laden, who wanted to keep Afghani women oppressed according to Islamic law.

After the Soviet invasion, the USA and its allies—the United Kingdom, Western Europe, Pakistan and Saudi Arabia—started financially supporting the Mujahedeen and Osama bin Laden's military to fight the Soviet Army and keep Afghan women oppressed and Afghanistan in political and social turmoil.

At center stage of all the turmoil and wars in Afghanistan in the past and in the present time was—the oppression and domination of women by men—this is the cornerstone of Islamic law. In the past Afghan women were not always oppressed by Islamic fundamentalism as it occurred today under the Mujahedeen and Taliban.[1]

North of Afghanistan was on the border of the USSR, or the Soviet Union, where 3 Soviet Union Muslim republics were located: Turkmenistan, Uzbekistan, and Tajikistan. There, all Muslim women had equal opportunity granted to them by the Russian Revolution of November 1917.

This historic event also had a profound impact on its neighbor, Afghanistan. After the Russian Revolution of 1917, Afghanistan was a peaceful Soviet neighbor that began promoting economic modernization and the emancipation of women in 2 different time periods.

The 1st period was the beginning of the 1920s. Veils and polygamy were abolished and the education of Afghani girls was installed.

Then the British, to keep Afghanistan in political, social, and economic turmoil, unveiled propaganda in the form of photographs, showing to Afghan tribal chiefs and mullahs in the rural area about women emancipation in Kabul. Tribal chiefs revolted and by the end of the 1920s, education for girls was abolished.

The 2nd period was the mid-1950s to 1992. Through massive foreign and economic assistance from the Soviet Union, Afghanistan went through a "cautious" modernization. Women again were encouraged to participate in their country's development. They became teachers, nurses, and doctors and in 1964, they were given the right to vote.

In 1965, the PDPA (People's Democratic Party of Afghanistan) came to power promoting socialism: mass literacy for all, opportunity for women, abolishing arranged marriages, and reforming land ownership.[1]

The same year, the DOAW (Democratic Organization of Afghan Women) was formed, advocating literacy among women, the prohibition of forced marriages, the bride prize, and the increase in the minimum marriage age to 16 years for girls and 18 years for boys.

The 1st woman Minister of Health was elected alongside 3 more women. In the 1970s, the Soviet Union supported regime moved the women's agenda to the center. Women were employed in universities and private companies and became professionals.

The emancipation of women in Afghanistan was considered a threat to neighboring Pakistan and their traditional Islamic tribal traditions. They started fighting the socialist regime, encouraging Afghan's Islamic leaders in rural areas to revolt. They did. Tribal chiefs and mullahs reverted to violence against women, shooting women in Western clothing, rebelling against women education, and killing PDPA reformers.

The USA stepped in with its allies—the United Kingdom, Western European, and Saudi Arabia—pouring billions of dollars to organize, train, and supply weapons to multi-national insurgents called the Mujahedeen to fight the emancipation of Afghan women.

"Freedom fighters" mushroomed and were fueled by funding and political interaction of the USA and its allies. The Mujahedeen formed its own army, a war in the name of Islam, which was a reversal of all gains of the social policies developed by the PDPA regarding women's equal rights.

The Soviet Union, sensing the PDPA's weakness, deployed the 40th Army into Afghanistan in December 1979. The war between the Soviet-led Afghan forces and Mujahedeen lasted for over 9 years; 15,000 Russian troops were killed and over 1 million Afghans.

The Soviets did not win the war and withdrew in February 1988. The war was referred to as "the Soviet Union's Vietnam War." After the Soviets withdrew, the PDPA regime continued to hold on until 1992, when the collapse of the Soviet Union left the regime without any help.

In 1992, the Mujahedeen took over Kabul and declared Afghanistan an Islamic state. Women were sent back into complete head-to-toe garments with a mesh-covered opening for their eyes only. That was only the beginning. The Mujahedeen barbarian regime burned down universities, libraries, and schools.

In 1996, with Pakistani military support and Saudi Arabian money, the Taliban occupied Kabul, cleansed the socialist government and transformed Afghanistan into an Islamic state forbidding women to attend schools, work, or leave their homes without male escorts.

They even set up a department to monitor and control women behavior according to Islamic law. By early 2001, the Taliban controlled 90% of pro-American Afghanistan. Osama bin Laden founded al-Qaeda in the late 1980s to support the Mujahedeen war against the Soviet Union and his brigade was responsible for mass killings of Afghan civilians.

The Soviet Union was fighting for a democratic Afghanistan, not Islamic. From the mid-1950s to 1992, Soviets emancipated Afghan women, installed mass education for the whole country, and women became teachers, nurses, and physicians.

They were able to vote, there were no arranged marriages, they worked outside of their homes, and they did not need a male family member to escort them everywhere outside their home. The emancipation of Afghan women gained from the 1950s–1992 was achieved by the PDPA, a socialist government financially and politically supported by the Soviet Union. In 1992 after the Soviet Union disintegrated, the emancipation of women was lost to the Mujahedeen and the Taliban, which was supported by the USA and it allies.

The USA and its allies spent billions of dollars helping Osama bin Laden and his Taliban to fight the Soviet Union in Afghanistan. The USA and its allies wanted Afghan women to follow strict Islamic laws where women had no rights, no education, were not allowed to drive cars, could be bought and sold, and were not allowed to vote. In short, women were second-class citizens.

Osama bin Laden and the Taliban were fighting barbarically the democratic socialist regime in Afghanistan, all to reverse the emancipation of Afghan women and reinstate the oppression and domination of women by men as the cornerstone of Islamic law.

In summary, the USA and its allies supported regimes that practiced the oppression of Afghan women and forced them to strictly follow Islamic law, where women had no rights, no education, were not allowed to vote or drive cars, and could be bought and sold; women were just merchandize.

The USA's usual policy in defending democracy and "human rights" was thrown out of the window. What kind of democracy and human rights was the USA applying to Afghan women?

The USA's actions supported aggression and authoritarianism regimes to fight the Soviets, regardless of what their objectives were. Even if the Soviets were savings elephants in Africa, the USA would have fought them over it.

Fate had a strange plan for the USA—their double standard policy backfired. Once Osama bin Laden's enemy, the Soviets, were gone in 1991, Osama bin Laden turned against his greatest military and financial supporter—the USA. He orchestrated an al-Qaeda terror attack on the World Trade Center and Pentagon on September 11, 2001. And started his Islamic holy war against the USA and Western way of life.

△ △ △

THE MORAL OF THE STORY

The Soviet Union established and supported a socialist regime in Afghanistan in the 1920s and then later from the mid-1950s to 1992. The regime gave Afghan women human rights and equal opportunity for many years.

To fight the Soviets, the USA, and its allies—the United Kingdom, Western Europe, Pakistan, and Saudi Arabia—interfered and spent billions of dollars helping the Mujahedeen, the Taliban, and Osama bin Laden to take away human rights from Afghan women and replace it with oppressive Islamic law.

What about Saudi Arabia today? It is one of the most oppressive Islamic nations in the world, and at the same time, a great friend and ally of the USA.

Afghanistan is a classic example where the USA pursued its double standard policy on "human rights." Looking for any disturbances in the world, the USA would support political, social, and economic turmoil or invade any country with only one objective: financial—to make money for their big donors—big corporations, banks, the military industry, and private contractors all while disregarding any "human rights."

The future of Afghan women is bleak without external help and financial aid. They continue to live impoverished and oppressed lives. It is doubtful that external help will ever come, when considering the present status reflected in the economic downturn of all developed nations in the West.

As for Afghanistan as a whole, with the explosion of its population, from 11.8 million in 1950, to 35.6 million in 2010, Afghanistan has little hope of halting its downward spiral.

---

[1] http://en.wikipedia.org/wiki/People's_Pemocratic_Party_of_Afghanistan
http://en.wikipedia.org/wiki/Soviet_war_in_Afghanistan
http://en.wikipedia.org/wiki/islamic_feminism
www.internationalist.org/afghanwomen1001.html

SHORT STORY

The Greatest Catastrophe of the 20th Century. Or, How the Soviet Union Disintegrated in 1991

A Person Is a Product of Time, Place, and Circumstances

△ △ △

"Only a donkey can assume that destruction of the [Soviet] union benefits anyone. The collapse of the Soviet Union would be a catastrophe for everyone."

Helmut Kohl, West German Chancellor from 1982–1990.

Why in the 1980s did no one see, predict, or ever think that such a great superpower as the 700-year-old Russian Empire—with its Soviet Union that conquered 1/3 of Europe and 1/2 of Asia —would suddenly disintegrate?

A) Why and How Did the Soviet Union Suddenly Disintegrate in 1991?

Why did the Soviet Union disintegrate? In 1991, the USA's and Western Europe's dreams and wishes to destroy the Soviet Union came true. The 700-year-old Russian Empire and world superpower, the Soviet Union, disintegrated, and socialism was gone.

The impact was global and as forceful as an earthquake measuring 10 on the Richter scale. Disintegration of the Soviet Union reshaped the whole world into a single system—the global capitalism.[1]

Ironically, the disintegration of the Soviet Union came back to haunt the USA and Western Europe; it has destroyed their economies and pushed the USA and Western Europe into economic decline.

The world today has become unstable and uncertain. Oil and raw resources are exhausted; ecological holocaust is booming, and the number of world millionaires and billionaires is growing.

At the same time, the majority of the people on the planet continue to become poorer, with income inequality becoming even more pervasive.

What Was the Soviet Union, or the USSR?

On November 6–7, 1917, the Russian Revolution, under the revolutionary leadership of Vladimir Ilyich Lenin, overthrew the Tsars (the Emperors), who has kept the Russian Empire backward and undeveloped.

The revolution transformed Russia into a new country governed by workers and peasants. On December 28, 1922, the USSR (the Union of Soviet Socialist Republics, or the Soviet Union), was created.

The USSR was not just simply a one monolithic country with a single Russian language. Instead, it consisted of 15 independent countries (republics), and it has 15 official languages.

In addition, it also had 15 smaller autonomous republics each with its own language. Each republic was governed as an independent country and had its own government. The primary language was a native one, and the 2nd language was Russian.

A Person Is a Product of Time, Place, and Circumstances

For example, the Georgian Republic had Georgian as the 1st official language, and the 2nd language was Russian. Or, let's take another example, the Azerbaijan Republic. Upon crossing from Russia into Azerbaijan, one would think he or she was in Iran—women covered their faces and were escorted by males, and mosques were everywhere. The Soviet Union had more Muslims than either Iran or Egypt.

After the Russian Revolution of November 1917, many decrees were issued. They were aimed at making the Soviet Union a democratic, free, and industrialized regime: peace decree; private land was nationalized and distributed to peasants; control of factories was given to the Soviet government; 8-hour workdays with higher wages were established; equal opportunity and equal rights for all were proclaimed.

Women were permitted not only to vote, but also to earn wages equal to men. Women received equal education, 4-month maternity leave, free child care, and rights to have abortions. Similarly, all citizens were given free health care, free education, free and inexpensive housing, safe working conditions, sick leave, 2–4 weeks paid vacation time, pensions for women at age 50 and for men at 55, and many more improvements in working and living conditions. The USSR was building a socialist society, and the country's economy had central planning characterized by production according to the needs of the people.

In the aftermath of the dissolution of a backward tsarist regime that had made up the provisional government, the USSR set out to industrialize itself into a modern country, initially establishing 5-year and 10-year industrial plans. Socialism succeeded and the USSR became strong, and the leader of socialism worldwide.

In 1939–1940, German and European Allied forces led by the Nazi Party leader Adolf Hitler occupied the whole Europe in just 3 months with little resistance.

On June 22, 1941, Hitler invaded the USSR, and World War II started. For the next 3 years, 1941–1944, the war was fought on Russian soil, and the Soviet Red Army was fighting Hitler's army. In June 1944, the Soviet Red Army liberated the USSR, pushed Hitler back, liberated Europe, and took Berlin, and on May 9, 1945, the Soviet Union announced World War II victory.

The Soviet Union won the war but at a catastrophic cost: 26.6 million Russians were killed, almost all men between the ages of 18 and 50. The entire country was in ruins; much of it has been leveled.

After the war, there were few men left to rebuild the country, so Russian women did. Working 2 shifts, they toiled in factories and on construction sites during the day; and at night they studied in schools and universities. Over the next 15 to 20 years, the Soviet Union was rebuilt and regained its influence.

A Person Is a Product of Time, Place, and Circumstances

By 1985, the Soviet Union was at the height of its global power and influence. It was a world superpower, and the leader of socialism. By then, many nations and regimes were under the umbrella of socialism: among them were China, India and Cuba. Joining the many socialist countries in Asia and South America were nations of Eastern Europe and in Africa. The Soviet society was educated, resourceful, and sophisticated.

Why and how did the Soviet Union suddenly disintegrate in 1991? Nothing happens by accident; there are always reasons for it. What was the political and social environment in the 1980s? What were the factors and circumstances responsible for the Soviet Union's disintegration?

Environment Before Disintegration

What were the political and social environments in the Soviet Union like at the beginning of the 1980s? All Soviet General Secretaries (Presidents) of the Central Committee of the Communist Party (Politburo) were selected based on their experience, nobility, wisdom, character traits, and their skills.

Before 1985, the Soviet Union had stoic, patriotic, and nationalistic General Secretaries. They were born before the Russian Revolution of November 1917, and they lived and worked during unstable, difficult, and challenging times.

They had faced problems of epic proportions: revolution, civil war, World War I, and World War II. They had to combat hunger, disease, and the postwar reconstruction of the Soviet Union with only able Russian women and old men.

The country was transformed from the backward Russian Empire of the Tsars into a world superpower. Every General Secretary was an "old guard" noble, brimming with nationalism and patriotism.

Their country, the Soviet Union, took precedent over their personal needs and wants. All the country's problems were solved, and by the 1980s, for the first time in its 68-year history, the Soviet Union was run as on automatic pilot.

There was an ongoing Cold War, but that was characterized by competition for technological progress and dominance of the world between the Soviet Union and the USA. These competitions produced space and military technology that spilled over to civilian industry and improved the quality of life of the populations of both nations.

By this time, the Russian population had become educated, sophisticated, and prosperous. The Russian people abandoned hundreds of thousands of villages and small towns and migrated to urban centers in search of industrial work, whereby they could live in new apartments and condos, and they could work, study, and entertain all in one place, a metropolis.

Hollywood Style Perception of American Capitalism

The socialist system was partly responsible for creating a Hollywood style perception of American capitalism among Soviet citizens.

Within the Soviet system, there was an internal danger to it from socialism's teachings and from Soviet postwar generations. The socialist system aimed to give the Soviet citizens the best free education, which in turn would create individuals of exceptional character.

That is why the Soviet population was not bombarded by propaganda, even as Americans were inciting hysteria of the prospect of nuclear attacks by Russians.

The Soviet government was not teaching Russians to hate Americans. Also, absent were drills for nuclear Armageddon, a fear mongering scenario, courtesy of America.

Quite the contrary, Russians loved Americans. Why? The best American movies, many of them, were shown in every city in the Soviet Union. The films had no subtitles; instead, American actors' voices were replaced by Russian actors' voices speaking Russian. Movies that the majority of Russians saw included: *Rhapsody, American Tragedy,*

Oklahoma!, 12 Angry Men, Gaslight, War and Peace, Breakfast at Tiffany's, Waterloo Bridge, Tarzan, Giant, Sun Valley Serenade, An Affair to Remember, A Streetcar Named Desire, and many more. And Russians saw many more movies from Europe and from all over the world.

The Russian post-war generation was lucky—they lived the good life. They enjoyed free education, health care, and housing; no unemployment, and 15–30 day paid vacations.

Many types of entertainment and libraries were accessible to everyone, who had at their disposal many thousands of the best books ever written by Russians and by international writers; these works were at their disposal; they were all translated into Russian.

It was their parents and grandparents who lived through the most difficult and challenging times in the Soviet Union's history: the Russian Revolution, Russian Civil War, World War I, and World War II. All their lives, people of these generations experienced tremendous suffering, sacrifice, hunger, and disease.

Now, in the post-war time, parents and grandparents wanted to give their children and grandchildren better lives than they had experienced.

The postwar generations were simply spoiled brats. The young adults were still living with their parents and

A Person Is a Product of Time, Place, and Circumstances

grandparents, paying them nothing; instead, they spent all their salaries on themselves.

Spending time at the movies, the opera, the ballet, and at plays; listening to philharmonic orchestras; reading the best books; wearing the best chic clothes and Italian leather shoes; dancing all night to rock 'n' roll; going to beach parties and taking sea cruises; eating in cafes and restaurants every day; attending international concerts and sporting events—these were common past times.

These young people also were grooming themselves well: every week getting manicures, pedicures, facials, hairdos, eyelashes, massages and spas treatments. Those services were cheap—subsidized by the government—and were located on every street corner.

Postwar generations spent time debating politics, and trends, and criticizing the Soviet government. The young Russian generations perception of American capitalism was acquired from the Hollywood movies and from music they danced to every night, including tunes by Glenn Miller Orchestra and Duke Ellington. Also popular was the music of Elvis Presley, and rock 'n' roll. The young people felt surely that, as in the movies, every American was a millionaire and lived in enormous wealth.

To suffocate the Soviet Union economically, the West had stopped having diplomatic relations and economic trade after the Russian Revolution of November 6–7, 1917. At the same time, the Soviet Union government did not allow their citizens to go abroad even on vacations. In order for a Russian to go abroad, one must defect.

That is why Russians having seen Western lives from the vintage point of foreign and Hollywood movies and mistook the fantasy for reality.

American history and literature were mandatory subjects in Soviet schools. The study of foreign language, either French or English, was mandatory starting in the 5th grade and continue through high school, with the same requirement as was for math, physics, chemistry, and other subjects.

Then, in universities, the study of French or English were also mandatory for 5 years. In short, a Russian student who failed French or English in school or in university, could not graduate.

As for classic and popular American and world writers, all were represented in every Russian school and public library. Russians also had private home collections with hardcover series of the classics by Russian and world writers. Books were cheap, and thus affordable for every citizen.

Russians by nature loved writers, poets, and musicians, and Russia is the most well-read nation in the world. When I was 8 or 9 years old, I started reading *The Adventures of Tom Sawyer and Huckleberry Finn*. I read all night and never stopped reading; I was hooked

A Person Is a Product of Time, Place, and Circumstances

on books, especially world classic books. My favorite American writer was Theodore Dreiser. In my home library, I had every book in his 12-books series in dark blue hardcover.

When I came to the USA and started telling my new American friends about my favorite American writers, few of them had ever heard about Theodore Dreiser, let alone read his 12 books.

In the Soviet Union, I also saw an American movie—*American Tragedy*—based on a Theodore Dreiser novel. The major heroine was played by my favorite actress, Elizabeth Taylor. The majority of Russians know her, as many had seen several movies she started in.

Americans who visited the Soviet Union were shocked to find that Russians loved Americans. Why didn't the Soviet leaders instill in their population hatred against Americans, as Americans leaders did against Russians?

Very simple. Tsarist Russia and the Soviet Union had conquered 1/3 of Europe and 1/2 of Asia and had under its empire more than 50 different nationalities. If the Soviet leaders had started promoting anti-American propaganda, such xenophobia could spill over to the other 50 or so nationalities in the Soviet Union.

That is why the attitude among Soviets during the height of the Cold War was not the same as that held by Americans toward Soviets. That is why there were no drills in preparation for an imaginary "American nuclear attack on Russians."

Moreover, socialism was building new kind of citizens—worldly, kind, and caring, not mean or aggressive, not circumspect, and not altogether self-centered.

The Crisis

What were the circumstances, crises and catalysts responsible for the Soviet Union's disintegration? Beginning in the 1980s, the circumstances of who ruled the Soviet Union drastically changed. In just a short period of over 2 years, November 1982–March 1985, one after another, 3 Soviet General Secretaries of the "old guard" generation died in sequential order one after another: Leonid Brezhnev, Yuri Andropov, and Konstantin Chernenko.

This was a crisis disrupting the country economically and politically and bringing about uncertainty.

What was the solution? The Central Committee of the Communist Party found the solution: it decided to select a much younger General Secretary, presumably one who would not die in office after several month. Based on age criteria, as opposed to leadership virtue, they chose 54-year-old Mikhail Gorbachev.

This bad selection sealed the fate of the Soviet Union. Little did the Soviet leaders know or expect that soon

A Person Is a Product of Time, Place, and Circumstances

Mikhail Gorbachev would disintegrate the Soviet Union, bring historic suffering to the Russian people, and usher in catastrophe to the world.

The Circumstances

The circumstances were the following.[1] The Soviet Union had bad luck when it selected General Secretary (President) Mikhail Gorbachev, who was ineffectual and characterless as a leader. Gorbachev (born 1931) was elected as General Secretary on March 11, 1985.

All of Gorbachev's predecessors were very busy focusing on solving epic and monumental problems of the Soviet Union in the 20th century: revolution, civil war, World War I, perception of an "Iron curtain," World War II, and the rebuilding that followed it, Cold War, and fulfilling 5-year and 10-year economic plans.

Previous leaders had no time or energy for experimentation. Also, they were the "old guard" generation: stoic, noble, and steeped in tradition and nationalistic virtues.

Gorbachev inherited a different Soviet Union. Its many monumental and challenging problems were all solved by his predecessors. The country was run on automatic pilot and was crisis free, for a change.

Having plenty of free time, looking for what to do and how to occupy himself, and pondering what legacy to leave behind, Gorbachev invented new social experiments such as "perestroika" (restructuring) and "glasnost" (openness).

They were failed experiments that collapsed the economy and destroyed the Soviet Union. Gorbachev's controlling wife, Raisa, was purported to be his closest confidant and the architect of all his policies; he took her everywhere he went.

His actions clearly indicated that he became a member of the Communist Party not to spread the party's ideology, but rather to fulfill a personal agenda. The majority of people in his and in later generations joined the Communist Party to advance personally if they lacked enough intellect or strong character to succeed on their own without the Communist Party's help.

With the strategic planning and policy advice of Raisa, Gorbachev started traveling to the West and the USA garnering acceptance. This achieved dual goals for Gorbachev: impressing Russians at home and propping up his low self-esteem by the West's acceptance.

He was parading his theories of "perestroika" and "glasnost" to his newly found friends, the West, and in particular, the USA.

At that time, I was working in Washington, D.C. and was driving between Washington, D.C. and Baltimore, Maryland. The local radio waves were occupied for many hours with Gorbachev's lectures. He delivered these in the Russian language to Americans, but no Americans were listening to him.

How many foreign presidents visiting Moscow were giving lectures to Russians in their native tongue endlessly occupying local radio waves? None, nobody, no one, ever. What was he up to?

He and his wife ingratiated themselves with Margaret Thatcher, the British Prime Minister, and an antagonist of the Soviet Union. Upon their return to the Soviet Union, the Gorbachevs were excited about having American Express cards and many fashionable clothes and shoes that they had purchased on their new credit cards in Western Europe. In her new Western clothing, Raisa started promenading herself as the "Jacqueline Kennedy of Russia."

Thatcher, seeing how weak the Gorbachevs were and how dependent both of them were on her acceptance, famously declared: "We can do business with Mr. Gorbachev."

President Ronald Reagan, having Gorbachev under his foot, and ahead of the world knew that Gorbachev was leading the disintegrating Soviet Union. In 1988, President Reagan, when standing in the Red Square in Moscow, declared that the "Evil Empire" (the Soviet Union) belonged to "another era."

For the West's acceptance of him, Gorbachev sold the Soviet Union to the West, and soon he announced: "We will not invade our satellite countries." This meant that the 700-year-old Russian Empire, and now the Soviet Union, could disintegrate. It did. The Eastern European countries outside the Soviet Union, and 30 Soviet republics inside, one by one, declared independence from the Soviet Union.

Gorbachev disintegrated the Soviet Union in parts:

> The 1st part: Gorbachev abandoned the Brezhnev Doctrine—the expansion of the Soviet Union power across the globe. Then, under guidance from President George H. W. Bush, signed the Geneva accord on April 14, 1988, reassuring the USA that he would withdraw troops from Afghanistan by February 15, 1989.
>
> The 2nd part: in 1989, Gorbachev announced that the Soviet Union would not interfere in Eastern European countries' affairs. The result was predictable. All Eastern Europe fell from the Soviet Eastern European orbit: Yugoslavia, Albania, Bulgaria, Poland, Romania, Hungary, Czechoslovakia, and Eastern Germany.
>
> The 3rd part: at the end, and by 1989, Gorbachev's ill-fated "glasnost" and "perestroika" had brought the Soviet Union to the point of no return. By the end of his reign, the country experienced a severe shortage of basic food: meat, flour, oil, and sugar. The war system of food distribution was introduced, giving each citizen a limited ration of food per month.

A Person Is a Product of Time, Place, and Circumstances

The 4th part: the Soviet Union's "inner empire" of 15 republics and 15 autonomous republics sought sovereignty, and then independence, from the Soviet Union. At the end of 1991, on December 25 Gorbachev called the White House and reported his achievement to his masters: "The Soviet Union has ceased to exist."

Gorbachev and his wife knew that they had destroyed the Soviet Union, and now came the day of reckoning—they must pay the price[2].

After 3 days of house arrest in their Crimean cottage (dacha), they both were escorted by airplane to Moscow. Being of weak character, inside of the airplane, they violently panicked and fell apart.

His wife Raisa was in worse condition than Gorbachev. Scared, she became mentally ill. Lying on the floor of the airplane, she became paralyzed on one side of her body and exhibited other manifestation of a breakdown of sorts. Her speech was impaired, and a stress-induced hematoma transformed her eyes into a bloody red color. In Moscow, the airport security could not coax her from the airplane. An ambulance was called, and she was sedated and transported to a hospital's mental ward.

I watched these events unfold. Both were cowards of low character. They each had a psychological meltdown and went out of their minds when they became fearful that the Russians would punish them for destroying the country.

Raisa was not the "Jacqueline Kennedy of Russia" as she had wanted to be called.

The Gorbachevs' mental instability revealed what bad luck and terrifying fate the Soviet Union had by having these kind of leaders—Gorbachev and Raisa—who were only parading around in the West, looking for attention and acceptance.

The Soviet Union had no chance of prosperity or continued its technological development, because the Gorbachevs stopped both.

And what did the Soviet Union's archrival and nemesis, Margaret Thatcher, want in return for her indulging the Gorbaches in sycophancy? She wanted—the dissolution of the Soviet Union. After meeting the pair, she realized they could be played, and play she did. Gorbachev and Raisa disintegrated the Soviet Union and brought catastrophe to the world.

Later, an unpublicized Gorbachev paper revealed the truth behind the Soviet Union collapse: Helmut Kohl, the West German Chancellor (1982–1990) at that time, in his last telephone conversation with Gorbachev as the General Secretary of the Soviet Union, stated: *"Only a donkey can assume that destruction of the [Soviet] union benefits anyone. The collapse of the Soviet Union would be a catastrophe for everyone."*

A Person Is a Product of Time, Place, and Circumstances

On December 25, 1991, the Soviet Union dissolution was complete and on that day Gorbachev sent a letter to Chancellor Kohl:

Dear Helmut!

Although the events did not go the way I felt would have been correct and most advantageous, I have not lost hope that the effort I began six years ago will eventually be concluded successfully, and that Russia and the other countries that are now part of a new community will transform themselves into modern and democratic countries.

With all our hearts, Raisa and I wish Hannelore (Kohl) and your entire family health, prosperity and happiness.

Your Mikhail.

And how did the West and the USA remunerated the Gorbachevs for disintegrating the 700-year-old Soviet Union Empire that millions of brave Russians sacrificed their lives to expand, defend, and save?

Once the West received from the Gorbachevs what it wanted, the former Soviet leader quickly receded into obscurity, and has been all but forgotten.

Gorbachev's dissolution of the Soviet Union did not go well for him personally. In his sunset years, at age 76, he went onto advertise ladies' luxury handbags made by the French fashion house of Louis Vuitton.[3]

In the back of a car, he was surrounded by ladies' bags. The Berlin Wall was pictured in the background, to remind people who he was and what he had done. It was not his 1st appearance in advertisements.

Years before, Gorbachev had appeared in television commercials for Pizza Hut and for an Austrian rail transport. Such was the rise and fall of Gorbachev—he went from being the former leader of the nation that comprises 1/6 of the world's territory to being a peddler of pizza.

But Gorbachev needed to make a living. He was no longer living in the Soviet Union for free, no longer part of a state that took care of each individual from cradle to grave. Here he was living in a capitalist world he was now gratuitous towards, so he had to go work hawking things that made a spectacle out of him. Isn't that what he had idealized?

He disintegrated the Soviet Union into capitalism, so that he and his wife could became rich and live a life of luxury. That did not materialize for them personally.

Instead, he became known as Gorbachev, the former Soviet president who was relegated to selling pizzas and Louise Vuitton handbags. What a risible sight to behold!

In summary, for the better part of the 20th century capitalism exemplified by the USA and Western Europe sought to destroy socialism typified by the Soviet Union.

By 1991, 2 psychologically unstable individuals, Mikhail Gorbachev and his controlling wife, Raisa—showed how to do it. They disintegrated the Soviet Union; it ceased to exist.

Status of the Former Soviet Union Immediately After Disintegration

I flew to see my relatives and friends after the Soviet Union disintegrated in 1991. Before going, I called and advised them of my arrival. To my surprise, they did not want me to visit them, saying that I must wait and come later.

Puzzled, I went anyway. They warned me that I must not fly to the airport in Odessa but instead to Kiev. At Odessa's airport, I risked harm because it was dangerous for me to be carrying an American passport.

I flew to Kiev, and from there I traveled by road to Odessa. Kiev at night was dark, all the streets were empty. Electricity apparently had ceased due to energy shortages in this city of 3 million people. I saw not a single inhabitant on the streets. "What happened?" I asked my friends. They explained that there was no money to pay for electricity. The electricity was switched off during the night and the majority of hours during the day.

Why had no one wanted me to fly in to see them in Odessa? Soon I found the answer. They were ashamed that I would see them in such dire straits as they had lost all sense of norms and decency; the rug had been pulled out from underneath their feet as they had lost virtually everything. Hospitals could not function; there was no equipment, no drugs, not even aspirin. Crime and violence skyrocketed overnight.

Before, the Soviet Union had had almost no crime, only 6 murders a year, and rape was almost unheard of, as were burglaries.

Now gangs and hooligans, along with Mafia groups, who patterned themselves after the movie *The Godfather*, flourished, holding all the population in fear. Life became like a jungle. There were no laws, no regulations, and police had no guns or cars. Human beings, once a safety net was removed, became violent criminals and members of the Mafia simply to survive.

In the 3 weeks I was there, I saw no milk, cheese, or any meat in the shops. Old grandmothers, who before had been the backbone of every Russian family, now became beggars on the streets. Grandmothers would sit on the pavement with outstretched hands asking for donations, as hundreds of people passed by without paying any attention to the begging.

Never before in human history had human beings on such a large scale—148 million people—suffered so much. Millions of Russian men age 50 and older died shortly after the dissolution of the Soviet Union.

The United Nation conducted a study: "Why Russian men aged 50 and older died?" The answer was simple—Russian men lost their breadwinner status and became poor. They were nobody; they had no present and no future. Dignity was taken from them, their dreams were shattered, and there was no desire to live.

After the Soviet Union collapsed, poverty became epidemic and the rule of law ceased to exist. Hyperinflation wiped their savings out overnight, and there were no pensions, no jobs, and no safety net.

The highly educated, stoic, and proud Russian nation was gone. There were no future and no dreams; their values, ideas, and pride had evaporated. Mass poverty now became a norm.

The majority of institutions were disbanded; factories and plants were closed. Now in charge were oligarchs who simply took over all national resources and state-owned assets by declaring these assets now in private hands—their own.

Criminals took factories, plants, oil refineries, mines, supermarkets, ports, trade ships, railways, transportation systems, government buildings—everything that could be pillaged and stolen was pillaged and stolen. Many in the lower class—former criminals and aspiring criminals—suddenly became rich, and some even millionaires and billionaires. The dramatic downturn and ensuing upheaval and chaos paralyzed the society.

Boris Yeltsin, a Successor of Gorbachev

The successor of Gorbachev was Boris Yeltsin (1931–2007).[4] In 1992, he assumed power as president of what now is Russia. A newly disclosed secret Gorbachev paper revealed Chancellor Kohl's thoughts on that development.

The following describes a telephone conversation between Chancellor Kohl of West Germany and Gorbachev:

Chancellor Kohl could not imagine that another catastrophe [after Gorbachev] was hanging over the Soviet Union—Boris Yeltsin, an unstable sick alcoholic. Kohl told Gorbachev:

"I have to say that the mere thought of it horrifies me. Of course that country cannot be left to such a man [Yeltsin]." Gorbachev responded: "We certainly agree on that level."

Chancellor Kohl's above trepidation became reality. After a coup to overthrow Gorbachev, Boris Yeltsin took power and became president of Russia on June 12, 1991.

Yeltsin was against Gorbachev and his "perestroika." Instead, he renamed the Kremlin the "White House," and burned the Communist Party, of which he was a member for 40 years. Yeltsin embarked to completely dismantle socialism and fully implement capitalism and to transform Russia's central planning economy into a free market economy; inherent in this was a near lethal dose of economic shock therapy by privatization of state assets.

He succeeded in his mission. The majority of Russia's national wealth fell into the hands of a small group of criminals, who became known as oligarchs.

One such example of "privatization" of national wealth that took place at that time was in Odessa. The Soviet Union had flotilla of 470 or so trade ships, which sailed from the port of Odessa on the Black Sea to destination all over the world. The ships were new, and they were equipped with the latest technology. They were the pride of the country.

One day, an announcement was made in Odessa that the following day an auction would take place to sell every government ship to private individuals. The general population stayed at home. It was scared and terrified of such an announcement. People knew that armed criminals would appear at the auction and commandeer it to bid and to buy.

The country became lawless and was ruled by the Mafia in partnership with corrupt government officials. Violent crime skyrocketed; murders and everyday shootings became the norm.

Criminals were in charge of these auctions. Bidding started, and not many bidders participated and not much money was involved. The ships were sold for $5–$20 each. With that, criminals, now turned new oligarchs, became instant millionaires and billionaires (each ship had a market value closer or above $1 billion).

Yeltsin immediately declared that he was changing Russia's socialist centrally planned economy into a capitalist free market economy. He had no idea what a market economy was and that no market economy could happen overnight. A market economy requires established laws and regulations already on the books.

For example, the USA, the paragon of the market economy, during its 200-year history had many laws and regulations on the books. Also, the Congress and the Senate were continuously designing new laws, and modifying or canceling old laws and regulations.

Even more, for a market economy to survive and function smoothly, those laws and regulations must be rigidly enforced. A complex system is in place in the USA: 1.1 million lawyers, with continued enrollment in American law colleges of around 140,000 law students in any academic year.

Hundreds of judges rule on these laws, and thousands of court houses and prison structures were built to try, convict, and house 2.2 million prisoners. How many police stations, police officers, police cars, helicopters, and weapons are in every small or big American town or city? Countless.

Overnight and incredulously, a market economy was imposed on a new, now "capitalist" Russia by the new President Yeltsin. Yet Russia had not 1 single market

A Person Is a Product of Time, Place, and Circumstances

economy law or regulation on the books, nor any system to enforce it, much less to rule on it. And no one even knew what the market economy was!

The Soviet Union, under a centrally planned economy, graduated fewer than 2,000 lawyers per year. They were practicing socialist law, not capitalist law. Like everything else in the Soviet Union, education was centrally planned. That determined how many lawyers were needed. There were few defense lawyers or juries, all because there was almost no crime.

Homes were often never locked. Any woman could walk 3–5 miles across the city after midnight, and never a thought would cross her mind that someone might rob, rape, or assault her. There was little crime, and thus no need for many criminal defense lawyers.

Why was there almost no crime in the Soviet Union? There was a generous safety net for everyone. There was no unemployment, and no one was sleeping under a bridge. The Constitution of the Soviet Union guaranteed all citizens equal opportunity, lifetime employment, free housing, free education, and free health care. Pensions for all, retirement age for women at age 50 and men at 55.

Russian police carried no guns (all firearms were forbidden, even today), and had few police cars, they mostly walked their beats instead of driving around in police cars. Police officers' major tasks were issuing tickets to jaywalkers and to admonish anyone caught publicly intoxicated. The drunkards were gathered together and sobered up by cleaning streets and parks for 1 week, all in full view of the passing public, and enduring public's jokes.

Like Gorbachev, Yeltsin should never have been the leader of the Soviet Union. He was an unstable alcoholic and sought to ingratiate himself with those outside Russia versus from those within, his constituents.

Yeltsin traveled extensively abroad and he was a big friend of President Bill Clinton. An unstable alcoholic, Yeltsin had volatile outbursts, was gaffe prone, and during the years of his presidency he consistently provoked ridicule from news media with his antics and odd behavior.

Yeltsin tried to kill himself in 1987 by cutting his chest; he bleed profusely, but survived. He fell from a bridge while drunk, blaming it on "perestroika," but survived. He had many near-fatal heart attacks, but survived.

He was drunk while giving a televised lecture in the USA; in an USA airport upon his arrival, he watered the plants by relieving himself in front of his entourage, and many reporters. This incident was broadcast on TV.

One night, during his visit to the USA, drunk and in his underwear, he was seen flagging cars on Pennsylvania Avenue in Washington, D.C. to buy pizza. Tragediante or comediante? To cry or to laugh?

Yeltsin's years were marked by high inflation, economic collapse, widespread corruption, and monumental political and social upheaval.

Between 1991–2000, Russia's growth shrank by 40%, a record for a country during peacetime. Some economists argue that, during the Yeltsin years, Russia suffered an economic downturn more severe than the USA's Great Depression in the 1930s.

Yeltsin received $40 billion in funds from the International Monetary Fund and other organizations to help its starving population, but all of those funds were stolen and pocketed by Yeltsin's inner circle, and parked in foreign banks. When leaving office on December 31, 1999, his approval rating was 2%. He was replaced by Vladimir Putin.

B). The Greatest Catastrophe of the 20th Century

Why was the dissolution of the Soviet Union one of the seminal events of the 20th century? The resultant upheaval and chaos that occurred left many worse off than before, in spite of promises that had been made to the contrary. Further, there was little time to adjust to this abrupt shock and reversal away from socialism as it happened suddenly, almost overnight, on December 25, 1991.

The dissolution of the Soviet Union changed the world into a single system—global capitalism and market economy. The unchecked speculative fever that resulted led the economies of USA and Western Europe downhill.

In 1991, the USA and Western Europe's dreams and wishes to destroy the Soviet Union and its socialism system came true. The 700-year-old Russian Empire and the world superpower Soviet Union now dissolved, the Soviet Union ceased to exist. Socialism was gone and like a magnitude 10 earthquake on the Richter scale, its shock waves reshaped the whole world into a single system—global capitalism with a free-market economy.

Today, under global capitalism, the rat race to become a millionaire and "get rich quick from thin air" is never ending. This has resulted in fierce competition for disappearing oil and raw resources, created an ecological near holocaust, and offered an abundant supply of cheap labor for multinational companies.

The number of millionaires and billionaires increases every year while the majority of people on the planet starve on stagnant or declining low wages.

Ironically, the adage "be careful what you wish for" now haunts the USA and Western Europe, as now unrestrained and unchallenged speculation has led to froth and bubbles that dwarf even the Dutch tulip mania of the 17th century.

Today, the USA is practically bankrupt having borrowed $19 trillion which it appears to pay back by the printing

A Person Is a Product of Time, Place, and Circumstances

of money. At the same time uses a hidden tax called inflation to wreak havoc on the savings of its people.

Today, Western Europe's economies also are broken, unemployment is up to 30% for youths, future generations denied a better life than their forebears, and countries are feasting on debt as a cure to solve a debt problem.

The burden of Western Europe's national debts now requires "austerity" from its citizens—or, a reverse "Robin Hood" government policy of imposing the hidden tax of inflation on its citizens, so that banks can be bailed out of a mess the banks themselves created. In turn, the population now experiences greater poverty and unemployment, higher suicides rates, and more protests.

Western Europe possesses no raw resources of its own, yet it is densely populated, with an average of 8,100 people per 1 square mile. It must buy oil and other raw resources on the world market, paying premium market prices and competing for them with 7.2 billion other people versus a population of 700 million before the Soviet Union disintegrated.

How is Russia, the Largest Part of the Former Soviet Union Doing Today?

It took more than 700-years to build the Russian Empire that then became the Soviet Union. Millions of Russians sacrificed and died to build and defend their lands.

Conversely, it took 2 "new guard" leaders—Gorbachev and Yeltsin—only several years to destroy the Soviet Union. The former had low self-esteem and was controlled by his unstable wife, and the later was a sick alcoholic with violent outbursts.

The tragic destiny of the Russian nation is colossal. Not one tragedy writer in the world ever could have predicted or foreseen a tragedy of such an epic scale in the Soviet Union disintegration; not William Shakespeare, nor Fyodor Dostoevsky.

Unfortunately, Gorbachev and Yeltsin were not fictional characters in Shakespeare or Dostoevsky's tragedies; they were real characters in the Russian national tragedy.

Before them was Grigori Rasputin, a Russian peasant, mystic healer, alcoholic, and womanizer who had a powerful influence over the last tsar of Russia as "the Mad Monk." He brought down the Romanov dynasty. Members of Russian aristocracy attempted to save the tsar's monarchy, and murdered Rasputin in 1916.

Today the Soviet Union is gone. What is left of it is now called Russia, one republic out of 30 before. After the Soviet Union disintegrated, the majority of Russian men age 50 and older soon died in despair. They had lost their status as breadwinners overnight.

Pensioners, veterans, and senior citizens also fell into despair, having witnessed the loss of everything that they and their comrades had fought to protect as the 20th century drew to a close.

Today, there are no dreams and no future. That is why the stoic, proud, and highly educated, and sophisticated Russian people—who in the past, saved the world and civilization 2 times (in 1812 from Napoleon, and in 1941–1945 from Hitler, World War II) are suffering now as no other nation has before.

Today, the majority of the Russian population lives in poverty; corruption is rampant on the same level as found in Africa and South America.[5]

The crime rate and drug consumption are higher in Russian than in the USA. Meanwhile, a small number of criminals, called oligarchs, who stole the Soviet Union's national wealth, now live in excessive luxury, indulging whims by buying extravagant mansions around the world and flying to them in their private jets.

Analysts and researchers call it "The quiet suicide of the Russian nation." By the mid-1990s, Russia's death rate had reached its highest peacetime level of the 20th century. Infectious diseases, such as tuberculosis, became a major cause of death, and rates of brucellosis and diphtheria doubled and quadrupled, respectively.

The rate of HIV/AIDS spread, and currently is among the highest in the world. Russians stopped reproducing. Even today, the Russian population is decreasing by 1 million per year.

There are twice as many deaths as there are births. By the year 2050, it is projected that the Russian population may fall from more than 148 million to 100 million.[5] By the end of the century, the Russian population will have disappeared from the face of the earth.

△ △ △

THE MORAL OF THE STORY

Why did the Soviet Union disintegrate in 1991? How did the disintegration of the Soviet Union bring near catastrophe to the entire world?

Secret Gorbachev papers revealed the truth behind the Soviet Union's collapse: Helmut Kohl, the West German Chancellor (1982–1990), in his last telephone conversation with Gorbachev as General Secretary of the Soviet Union stated:

"Only a donkey can assume that destruction of the [Soviet] union benefits anyone. The collapse of the Soviet Union would be a catastrophe for everyone."

A Person Is a Product of Time, Place, and Circumstances

For a large part of the 20th century, capitalism primary in the USA and Western Europe sought to destroy socialism and the Soviet Union. Then in 1991, 2 psychologically unstable people of low self-esteem—Mikhail Gorbachev and his controlling wife, Raisa demonstrated how to do it.

They disintegrated the Soviet Union—it ceased to exist. Disintegration of the Soviet Union brought historic suffering to the Russian people, pushed the USA and Western Europe down the hill, and brought catastrophe to the entire world.

Before the Soviet Union disintegrated in 1991, the world was in equilibrium and simple with 2 systems: capitalism and socialism. Competition between them led to innovation and improved the quality of life on the planet.

The capitalism system leader was the USA, whom Western Europe, Japan and Canada followed faithfully. The 700 million people residing in these nations represented the only demand on the world market for oil and raw resources; oil was below $20 per barrel before the dissolution of the Soviet Union, then it went shapely up.

The socialism system was led by the Soviet Union and under its umbrella were Eastern Europe, China, India, Cuba, and socialist countries in

Asia, Africa, and South America. These countries lived below their means thus having no demand for oil or raw resources sold on the world market.

For example, China, before the Soviet Union disintegration, was a socialist country, where people lived below their means, had almost no private cars, did not trade or buy raw resources on the world market, and had no millionaires. Today China has 2.4 million new millionaires and 152 billionaires, #2 behind the USA. In 2013, China's millionaire growth skyrocketed 82% from 2012, while the USA grew only 18% in 2013.

Today, the Chinese (1.4 billion population) are buying oil and raw resources sold on world market at a feverish rate, producing and buying more cars than the USA, and exporting cheap products and goods to the USA.

Today China is the #1 economy in the world as measured in purchasing power parity. Where do the Chinese and other countries get money to buy consumer goods? They do so by working in sweatshops and doing the low-skilled, low-paying jobs that were exported from the USA into their country.

In 1991, the USA's wish came true—the Soviet Union collapsed. There was no more Cold War

A Person Is a Product of Time, Place, and Circumstances

with the Soviet Union, no more "Evil Empire," no more exhorting of "Mr. Gorbachev tear down this wall [Berlin's wall]."

The Soviet Union disintegrated and the former socialist countries and continents, represented by Russia, China, India, Africa, and South America, all were left to fend for themselves—as newly minted capitalists.

The Soviet Union dissolution was a curse and not a blessing for the USA and Western Europe—their economies eventually spiraled down due to rampant laws of a free-market economy, categorized by "expansion in all direction without any restrictions."

Iceland, Greece, Spain, Italy and all other European countries teeter along as zombie states that have no oil, and no raw resources and must live under austerity, leading to joblessness and despair.

Today the whole world lives under one single system alone—the global capitalism system, and 7.2 billion inhabitants from over 195 countries seek an ever-larger slice of an ever-shrinking pie.

Today, everyone in the world wants "to get rich quick from thin air." Most notably, the vanguard of capitalism, the USA, seeks to promote the virtues of borrow now and pay later by exporting its currency used in international trade; thereby, imposing a hidden tax—inflation—on the meager pay and low wages of the 99% who were neither endowed nor plain lucky to be rich.

Even more, with the dissolution of the Soviet Union no longer was their any check or balances to wide-eyed speculations and risk taking in the pursuit of greed and selfishness, as single economy—global capitalism, or the "get rich quick from thin air" mindset has now taken root.

Today in the USA the middle class, (or working class) has disappeared, with many living in poverty or close to the poverty line; the national debt is over $19 trillion, and personal debt is over $17 trillion. Asian countries are rising, and Western countries are in decline.

Oil and natural resources are disappearing. Further, the demands of overpopulation on Earth has created ecological disaster, climate change, and pollution. The planet is in peril from overpopulation and from the impending ecological holocaust.

The Soviet Union disintegrated in 1991 and reshaped the world into a single system—global capitalism.

When were peoples' lives better? Before 1991? Or today? How can today global capitalism survive economic, environmental, and overpopulation catastrophes? Is there a future for the planet under the current single global capitalist system?

---

[1] http://en.wikipedia.org/wiki/Superpower
http://en.wikipedia.org/wiki/Mikhail_Gorbachev

[2] "The Gorbachev Papers: Secret Papers Reveal Truth Behind Soviet Collapse," by Christian Neef, Stratrisks.

"Everything You Think You Know About the Collapse of the Soviet Union Is Wrong," article by Leon Aron, 06/20/2011.

[3] "Mikhail Gorbachev Does Louis Vuitton," article published on November 28, 2007 in Culture magazine.

[4] http://encyclopedia.thefreedictionary.com/Boris+Yeltsin

[5] Russian mortality links: Data Summary of STIs, HIV, AIDs in Russia; Global Fund report for Russia, 2004.

SHORT STORY

It Is Easy to Despair, but the Best Traits of the Human Character Are Not to Give Up. But Instead to Stand Up, Fight Back, and Save Yourself

△ △ △

A Dream

It was the beginning of the 1980s. I had a dream. To get my doctoral degree, or PhD, to enhance my knowledge and become a better person.

At that time, my record of professional contributions was extensive; and I had no difficulty being accepted into any doctoral program of my choice. I designed many different structures that created national wealth, such as buildings, factories, bridges, and a subway on 3 different continents—the Soviet Union, Africa (Rwanda and Tanzania) and the USA—all under 3 different systems (socialism, the mixed economy, and capitalism), and in 3 different languages (Russian, French, and English).

I received a letter from the doctoral committee from the university of my choice congratulating me and informing me that I had been accepted as a doctoral candidate into the field of Management of Science, Technology and Innovations.

Hostile Environment to Women

Then, 1–2 weeks later I received another letter, this time from the Chairman of the department. His letter warned that: "Even though the Doctoral Committee has accepted you into our program, here [his department] we are prejudiced [against women]. Make your own conclusions." I still have his letter. Surprised, I did not know what to make of it. What should I do? My survival instincts dictated that I should keep quiet and not aggravate them.

Soon, I learned from other students that, before me, there was another woman, a doctoral candidate in his department. She did not survive long; in fact, they failed her. She was an American and I was a Russian during the Cold War between the USA and the Soviet Union.

Also, I came across another puzzle. At that time, every semester, approximately 40 new doctoral candidates, or 80 in total per year, were accepted to different doctoral programs at the school.

At the same time, only 1–2 dissertations, or none, were scheduled each semester for final defense. What happened to the rest of the candidates?

Did they just give up and leave? Later, I learned that a dissertation was simply no more or no less than just that—an innovation that was considered to be a new contribution to knowledge.

That was, a doctoral candidate had to create a new innovation (idea), and then develop it into a dissertation research project. Only those who had the creativity skills were able to design an innovation, and then develop it into a dissertation research project and graduate.

A Change in the Final Exam Rules: From Written to Oral

Soon 2 years passed, during which time I took and passed all of the required courses, labs, projects and essays, and was cleared to take the 3-day written final exam. If I passed the final exam, that would clear me to the next level—dissertation research. That did not happen.

When my time came to take the final exam, the university changed the rules. Now, for the 1st time in the history of the university, candidates were required to take an oral exam, instead of the usual 3-day written exam.

They changed the rule especially for me, to fail me. Their strategy was that if I took a 3-day written exam and they failed me, there would be a record of my answers. I could have asked an independent examiner to review and re-evaluate my answers and their mark.

On the other hand, if I took an oral exam, standing next to a blackboard answering their exam questions, there would be no record of my answers. How could I prove that I passed the oral exam? I could not.

Furthermore, the doctoral department was not even covering up why they had suddenly changed the rule to have an oral exam. They explained to other candidates that they "...Wanted to see the difference between a woman [me, Alla] and men," as if they could not see the difference by comparing written exams.

All the male doctoral candidates got scared. Never before had they taken a final exam in oral form. They knew the oral exam was designed especially to fail me and encouraged me to file a discrimination suit. And those who were unfortunate and had to take the oral exam at the same time as I did—panic. Some took a leave of absence, others asked their companies to transfer them to far away states. None of them took the risk.

As for me, what were my alternatives? I had none. To file a discrimination suit as some of the candidates suggested? I ruled that out. I entered the doctoral program to receive my PhD. Even if I did file a suit and won, how would that have helped me to pass the final exam, or design an innovation and then defend my dissertation? Down the road, they had many more opportunities to fail me.

The Final Oral Exam

I took a risk and started preparing for my final oral exam. The date was set up and by then, I was ready.

What my tormentors did not know was that I was a pro at taking oral exams. I finished a school and a civil engineering university in the Soviet Union where all the exams were oral, except math and the Russian language. Multiple choice exams did not exist. Analogy: It was as if they punished a fish by throwing her back into the water.

The day of my oral exam arrived. Standing next to the blackboard, I answered all their questions orally, or by writing my answers on the blackboard. I could only guess that my oral answers were so good that it evoked some flicker of dignity and honor in my tormentors. It seemed that they could not bring themselves to fabricate that I failed my final oral exam. I passed. They issued an order that cleared me to my next step, the dissertation research.

Next semester, the university reverted back to its usual rules, and the final exams were again 3-day written exams. The life start going on as if nothing happened.

I was happy go lucky, prematurely and naively assuming that all manufactured tricks to fail me were now behind me. In the next year there were 2 more attempts to fail me. This time they came from the Dean's department.

Dissertation Proposal

In the meantime, I designed ideas/innovations and started my dissertation research that the dissertation committee was likely to approve. The committee was assembled from university professors and from outside corporations, including their chief engineers, who were experts in Science, Technology, and Innovations.

The dissertation had a 2-part defense. The 1st part was a dissertation proposal. The 2nd part was a final public dissertation defense.

One day I was ready, and my oral dissertation proposal started. I was standing next to a blackboard and was answering the questions from the members of the committee. Each member had my proposal's synopsis on 160 bound pages in front of them.

The 1st part of my presentation went all right. Then, one of the committee members, Doctor Closley (not his real name), an Assistant Dean, stood up and literally ambushed me. In his long speech, he not only criticized my proposal, but even worse, he dismissed it completely, repeating many times: "She does not know what she is doing."

Stunned, I questioned myself. What did I do wrong? What did he know about my innovations that I did not? Until now I had a perfect record of innovations.

Everything I had designed before (buildings, factories, bridges, and subway) was all correct; they never crumbled or failed. What had happened now, what error had I made? Confused and puzzled by his ambush, I did not challenge him, nor did I fight back.

I was an honest professional. I did not lie, or manipulate the facts, let alone fabricate something to hurt or destroy another person. Such scams did not exist in my engineering profession. Until that point, I believed that Dr. Closley had found a fundamental error in my proposal that I had no clue about. I took him seriously as an honest and dignified professor. I swallowed the fruit from his poisonous tree, and as a sheep, without any resistance, I went directly into Dr. Closley's slaughter house.

However, the rest of the committee disagreed with his statement that "She does not know what she is doing." The result was that I had to do more research in certain areas. That was the typical procedure for all proposals. No one's proposal had ever been accepted 100% on the 1st go.

But, in my case, I had again to re-defend my dissertation proposal for the 2nd time. I did.

During my 2nd proposal defense, Dr. Closley kept quiet and made no more threatening objections to my proposal. My proposal was accepted and cleared for the next and final level, the final public dissertation defense. I was happy again and my dream to receive my doctoral degree was in reach.

Final Public Dissertation Defense

The day of my final public dissertation defense arrived. The dissertation committee all assembled at their desks, and in front of each of them was the labor of my hard work, my over 400 page final dissertation in a bound book. Students came in.

I was standing next to the blackboard answering their questions. Everything was going fine until it was Dr. Closley's turn. Suddenly, he made a dramatic move. He took my entire 400-page plus dissertation and threw it high into the air. Gravity made it drop back on his desk, which wobbled on its impact. He paused for some time to make sure that his dramatic flair registered in the minds of all the people in the auditorium. Then, he went in for the kill.

He turned to me and went ballistic, yelling and screaming at me: "Alla, your entire dissertation is biased! There is no contribution to knowledge in your dissertation! You are an engineer and you undertook your research in engineering! It is all biased!" He then dropped back in his chair, pleased with himself. He started scanning the room, enjoying the impression his dramatic act had made on everybody.

During his outburst, my knees trembled and nausea set in. I was in despair, I thought: "It is the end! He failed me again! It is not fair! My dissertation is great; there is nothing wrong with it!" I assumed that he was not acting alone, I was sure he received an order from his superiors and the Dean himself to fail me. "That is why he has manufactured this new scheme to fail me!" Those thoughts, with the speed of light, zipped across my mind.

"No! No! No! This time I am not going to allow him to fail me!" Adrenaline filled up my body with anger and fight. I jumped up and lashed back at him.

Me: "Dr. Closley, let me ask you, what is the name of your field?"

Dr. Closley: "My field is (he gave the name)."

Me: "So, you do research, analysis, write expert articles and books in your field, and field in which you are an expert? Do you do research or write expert articles in another field that is not familiar to you? For example, on disadvantaged children?"

Now Dr. Closley understood where I was going. His face turned red as a lobster, and he did not answer my question.

Me: (By now my voice was high-pitched and my hands were in the air, as I continued to bombard him). "I understand and agree with you, that if I were to undertake my dissertation research on chromosomes, there will be no bias. But! But! The level of my ignorance would be 100%!"

To diffuse the situation, my dissertation chairman immediately took over with a series of research questions. Everything had an end and was also applicable to my dissertation defense. By noon it was over. The questions stopped. I was told to leave the auditorium so the committee could start discussing my dissertation and then vote.

I was in the long corridor, alone and pacing back and forth just to pass the time. What did I feel? Nothing—just emptiness. I had no emotion. I did not care whether I passed or I failed at that point. I only felt one kind of emotion: antipathy. I was disgusted.

Why was life so unfair? Why had I spent 3.5 years of my life working 24/7 everyday on a dream to get my doctoral degree? During those years, I was isolated from life and the world. I had no idea what was going on around me; I never read the newspaper, watched TV, or noticed seasonal changes. My focus, my heart and mind, like a beam, was concentrated only on one objective, my doctoral degree. Was it the worst? I did not think so.

Had I known beforehand that I would have to go through such ignorance, prejudice, and suffering, I would never even have dreamed to attempt it.

Regardless of how good of a doctoral candidate I was, or whether my dissertation was the best, there were professors who wanted to fail me, just because I was a woman. Ignorance and prejudice ran rampant in the universities.

During that time in the news, the media sometimes claimed that American universities were the last battleground for equal opportunity for women. Male professors and university administrations were to blame.

After 40–45 minutes passed, I was called back into the auditorium to hear my dissertation verdict. I was calm and had no feeling. My heart was empty. I did not care. The dissertation chairman took the stand.

He 1st apologized for keeping me so long in the corridor. He explained that my dissertation was great and they accepted it 100% without ordering any more additional research or changes. Because of that, they did not have a specific form to fill in for a dissertation that required no additional research. So they called some other universities, asking their advice as to what to do.

They liked my research and my oral answers. My written English was excellent, but there were some Russian words that needed to be edited. They had an editor, and she would edit it in several days. And that was it. I was ready for graduation that was already scheduled for all university students in 2 months.

Later, the chairman of my dissertation wrote that my dissertation was ranked the top 5% of the 250–300 dissertations written in the last 15 years.

From my above personal example, one can draw the conclusion that:

1) During my 1st attempt at the dissertation proposal, Dr. Closley, in advance, created a scheme to fail me. Then, to implement his scheme, he addressed my dissertation committee at the same time he ambushed me with his verdict "She does not know what she is doing." Astonished and frightened, thinking that something was indeed wrong with my dissertation proposal, I did not challenge him, nor did I fight back. Like a sheep, I accepted his false claim.

2) That was not over. During my final dissertation defense, Dr. Closley again crafted a new scheme. This time he threw my dissertation, over 400 pages of it, into the air, declaring that "It is all biased! There is no contribution to knowledge here!" This time I recognized that it was déjà vu all over again.

He did not care about the quality of my dissertation; rather, he was pursuing his personal agenda and prejudice. Now I discovered his real intention. I was a woman, a Russian, and he did not want any women to receive a PhD.

This time I did not go, as a sheep, into his slaughterhouse. I did not go into despair, as I did the 1st time. Instead, I stood up and fought back. This time, I won and he lost.

If I had not stood up to Dr. Closley during my final dissertation defense and instead accepted his contrived scheme to fail me, indeed I would have failed, and I would have never achieved my dream, of completing a doctoral degree.

The twist of fate. Dr. Closley spent 1.5 year of his life crafting, pursuing, and imposing his personal agenda to flank me, to humiliate me, to destroy my life and make sure that I would never achieve my goal and receive my doctoral degree. Little did he know that at the same time, fate had different plans in store for him. The next time I met the Dean and asked him about his assistant, he gave me shocking news. Dr. Closley died from cancer.

△ △ △
THE MORAL OF THE STORY

When someone crafting schemes to fail you, or pursuing his or her personal agenda to humiliate you, or make your life difficult—challenge him or her.

Remember, it is easy to despair, but the best trait of human character is not to give up, but instead to stand up, fight back, and save yourself.

SHORT STORY

A Fly in a Bottle.
Or, If Only I Knew it Before

A Person Is a Product of Time, Place, and Circumstances

△ △ △

"If only I knew it before!" Many times in my life, I repeatedly whispered this phrase to myself. If only someone had shown me the way out, told me this information, or taught me those skills, I would be a different person and have a better life. Instead, I was like a fly trapped in a narrow-neck bottle.

I once saw a fly trapped inside a glass bottle, frantically bumping her body hundreds of times into the glass wall, flying in circles, desperately trying to find an exit and fly out. Exhausted, she could not figure out that she should fly through the narrow neck of the bottle, the nearby exit that separated her from freedom.

Hungry, without food and water, weak and badly injured, in the end, she fell to the bottom of the bottle and died. If only she knew about the exit, or had someone to guide her, then her life would not have ended.

Sometimes I feel exactly the same way, like the fly in the bottle, desperately knocking on many doors, trying to find an exit from an impossible situation, and asking for help to solve my problems.

I wasted a lot of energy, time, and money trying to open many inapplicable doors or solve new problems, realizing in the end how unsuccessful these efforts were and how much it would cost me. But, if from the beginning I had been armed with the needed information, knowledge, and skills about what to do and where to go, my efforts could have had different outcomes.

A vivid example of this was when I filed for divorce. It seemed like the whole world was crashing down upon me, testing my ignorance, unpreparedness, and lack of many street skills. Simultaneously, I was forced to deal with dozens of different firms and people. They all were from fields I had never dealt with before and barely knew, so the level of my ignorance was close to 100%. There were lawyers, courts, judges, accountants, experts, estimators, real estate agents, contractors, and subcontractors to renovate and sell our family's 20-year-old house.

The next 3 weeks were hectic and scary. I was like the fly trapped inside the glass bottle and had no idea where the exit was to fly out to freedom, in this case, from my monumental problems.

Panicky, confused, and crushed, one evening I retreated into a quiet place, my bed, and began taking a long inventory of my pending problems in the hopes of retrieving from my mind some solutions.

But I could not calm myself from all the problems I encountered during the day; my mind was still running in high gear calling for more actions, not calm. I reached for the telephone and called my eldest son in Philadelphia, a student at the University of Pennsylvania's Wharton School of Business.

A Person Is a Product of Time, Place, and Circumstances

Like a drama queen, in one paragraph I threw all my problems into his corner. "You know," I said, "You wouldn't believe what luck I've had! In the last 3 weeks it seems like everyone I met was a crook! Can you imagine such bad luck? They lie and manipulate and take advantage of me and my ignorance. Everyone is determined to make money from my vulnerability, problems, ignorance, and unfortunate situation."

For a long minute there was silence on the other end of the line. Then calmly, listening and weighing every word, my son gave me his answer: "Mom, listen, everyone you are dealing with now is indeed a crook. You are so naive, like a child. You are an engineer and see the world only in 2 dimensions: black and white. To you, everything has only 2 possible answers: it is right or wrong. It is simple, the engineering world. Now you have stepped into the business world. The business world does not have only 2 simple answers for any problem, as engineering does. The business world is a gray area; there is no definite right or wrong answer and anyone can stretch gray in any direction he wants." He spoke like my grandfather, who was a very wise man and he gave a simple logical explanation for all my problems.

I was glad I made that call: there was a simple explanation to my "bad luck"—all life lived is life learned. Curious as a child, excited to face new challenges and make new learning discoveries about the new world—the business world—I became a sponge with a new mission.

I now stepped into the new and unfamiliar territories of lawyers, courts, experts, accountants, estimators, contractors, subcontractors, and real estate agents. With minimum energy and in the shortest time, I acquired new information, skills, and knowledge, and helped myself.

△ △ △

THE MORAL OF THE STORY

One may indeed feel like a fly in a bottle when life sends new challenges and difficult problems to solve to someone who has no idea how to deal with them; especially when someone has never been in such a situation before. But there is very little one can do about it except to not despair from life's overwhelming problems.

Look at it as a challenge—an opportunity to learn, grow, and became stronger. Reach out for help, ask people, read books, and learn how to help yourself to solve all your pressing problems as soon as possible. Life is not static, it is dynamic. Even more, all life lived is life learned.

SHORT STORY

Return of the Sound. Or, Shocking News

△ △ △

There is no sound around me. Nope. None. Dead silence. Only my vision is engaged.

I sit still in the back of a long L-shaped room, looking straight through the big clear window. A misty panorama of the city, as from Greek mythology, appears in front of me.

On the top of the hill I see some distinctive high-rise buildings profoundly fencing the horizon. A shallow valley, like a guard, stands between me and the town. Hundreds of undistinguished small buildings, as wooden soldiers on a checker board, fill the slopes of the valley.

Rust-colored roofs wallpaper the town. Above the roofs, in some places, the morning fog has not burned yet and its milky content still hangs in the air.

Through the corner of my right eye, I see a long wall. Along the wall there is a door, a grey stand for the water cooler, a bin of cups, and 2 faucets. One faucet is a bright, illuminating blue.

My left eye has a much wider view, almost a 90-degree spectrum. It scans that side of the room, registering T-shaped rows of light and plastic chairs with a dozen people sitting in them. The chairs stop at the hub of the room's activities, a white counter.

Behind the counter, long vertical blinds cover the windows. The blinds have been opened at a skewed angle to restrict total exposure to the sun. Still the sun beams intensely through the openings, filling the top of the room with sunshine and lighting up a stream of dust near the floor.

The top of the room has no obstacles. Here the sun creates magic. It forms a rainbow beam of many colors. The rainbow wrapped in a foggy veil streams across the room, tranquil and undisturbed.

The bottom of the room is jumbled. Here sunshine constantly bounces and bumps into obstacles, creating a kaleidoscope of changing colors and shapes. People move, sparks fly in all directions, and the kaleidoscope breaks into fragments. The dust begins to burn through the rainbow.

Check the room for sound again. Nope. None. But now I detect motions. Some women are reading. One woman stands and moves toward the counter, another sorts out her purse. The only man there stretches his legs.

Diagonally, several feet from me, is a woman's profile. She holds a book, not on her lap but in the air, closer to her eyes. Perhaps she needs stronger glasses.

A young child appears in front of the water cooler. From his movements, I can tell that he is struggling to hold the triangular cup straight.

I am not frightened, even though there is no sound around me. Everything looks familiar; I have seen it many times before. Where? In my dreams? Watching silent movies?

I turn my attention outside. Not far from me, a major traffic artery crosses town. A sea of cars, like tiny matchboxes, lines up in a serpentine formation. The scenery is also familiar.

What town is this? My mind pressed for the answer. It is Towson, Maryland! Now, I notice, my mind is engaging. The sun is vivid.

From its position in the sky, I register the time of the day. It is around 11 o'clock in the morning. The town spreads for miles in all directions.

"At last," I thought happily. *"I detect sound!"* Indeed, I hear the sound that I have desperately been searching and waiting for. It is far away, near the horizon, on the top of the hill, somewhere behind the high-rise buildings.

I locate the sound. It originates from a small, dark dot. The dot, like a projector, releases a cylindrical beam. As if it were thunder, the beam disseminates thousands of amplifying sounds. It grows in intensity and rapidly closes the gap between us.

It zeros in on me. I feel the sound's magnetic field. I am frightened. Like a jungle at night, the amplifier drums up thousands of sounds that compete with each other.

A Person Is a Product of Time, Place, and Circumstances

The situation is beyond my control. Frozen, I watch in horror as the wall of sound rolls in my direction. Closer and closer. It hits me and my body reacts violently.

My glands produce intensive sweat and heat, and my clothes are quickly soaked. My head spins like a merry-go-round. No breath, gasping for some air. Call for help with numb lips and wooden tongue.

The room drums up the amplifier sounds of a jungle at night. My eardrums are cracking. *It is awful to be alive*, brushes through my mind. Dizziness is overwhelming. I throw up on my lap. Relief. The amplifying sounds taper off.

I know where I am now. I am in the waiting room of the radiology center. Just 5 minutes ago, they found something in my left breast. I am recovering from the shock and am back to real life. I grab my jacket and press it into my wet lap.

After a moment, I slowly navigate the room, ashamed to face someone who might have witnessed my experience. Nope. Nobody. No one. The same patients and some new ones engage in typical waiting-room activities.

Life was going on as if nothing happened!

I smile and giggle. Light tears fill my eyes. I hesitate a moment. Then pick myself up and quietly tiptoe to the exit. Open the door, and step into the parking lot.

THE MORAL OF THE STORY

A mammogram test gave me bad news. I was in a shock and semi-fainted. But... Life around me was going on as if nothing happened!

Stunned by such cruelty of life, I recognized, with the speed of light, that I am just a grain of sand, a short flash in the universe. Regardless of what happens to me, life goes on without stopping.

My sadness and my expectation that other people would feel sorry for me made me weak, selfish, and desperate. I should direct my energy to strengthen myself.

A dignifying lesson hits me: it is easy to despair and to trail behind. But the best trait of humanity is not to accept the situation, but to fight back. Pick yourself up and rally with the powerful force of life.

#15 SHORT STORY

Ability Is Nothing Without Opportunity

△ △ △

"Ability is nothing without opportunity"
Napoleon Bonaparte

Opportunity

For decades, I was given an opportunity to use my skills and creativity in my work. I never had a problem to getting a job; any company I applied to, I was hired and accepted.

There I created many innovations and made huge contributions to my profession, society, and the country, same examples of which are found through this trilogy in some of my short stories.

Then, my employment luck was abruptly shut down, and no one had any interest in hiring me. Why? What happened?

No Opportunity

In 1998, I left the East Coast and moved to San Francisco. I believed that with my implemented record of innovations and contributions in engineering and in health care, I would have no problem finding any job I wanted; companies would be competing to hire me. That never happened.

When I applied to any position, to my surprise, no one answered me. It was a mystery and a puzzle. What had happened? I could not figure it out.

By that time in my career, I had no resume; instead I had a record, a list of my huge contributions to companies, where my projects and innovations brought and continued to bring companies new revenue in the hundreds of millions of dollars every month.

The mystery started unraveling when one tax accountant, impressed by my innovations in health care, invited me to his board meeting. He was excited that I already had a solution to the problem they were trying to solve concerning Medicare.

Before, in another health care organization, I had already solved the same problem and I had given him blue print of my innovations for this solution. He told me that 1 small health care organization in Silicon Valley, where the majority of patients have Medicare, was running in the red.

To turn it around, a $2 million fund was established and this money had been given to a board to turn around this health care organization. A new board of outsiders was assembled, consisting of friends who know each other previously. Once the board became in charge of the $2 million fund, they created new positions among themselves, accompanied by huge monthly salaries.

My new friend, the accountant, was on the board and had received the position of CFO (Chief Financial Officer); one of his friends on the board had invited him to join their board. To complement his new position, he bought a bright new black Mercedes and the next day drove me to his board meeting.

There, he enthusiastically introduced me to his board, then asked me to describe how I was going to solve their Medicare problems.

I did, telling them that I had the expertise, a proven solution, and a blueprint from my previous innovation that could be used in their case. It would definitely turn this health care organization from red into black.

Even more, I promised them that it would take me weeks, not months to solve the problems. The board members expressed no enthusiasm in my ready solution, and they answered with silence and stony faces.

Baffled by their cold response, but still in an excited mood to get my hands on the problem as soon as possible, I asked to see the accounts receivable department and familiarize myself with their problems.

My new friend, the CFO of the board, called an account receivable manager to come up to the meeting room to escort me to his department. Strangely, the president of the board also left the meeting room and started shadowing me, following every step I took without uttering a single word.

When I had finished familiarizing myself with the department, I returned back to the meeting room. There,

A Person Is a Product of Time, Place, and Circumstances

a lunch was in progress. The board had arranged for food to be delivered to the premises in advance.

During lunch, I had an opportunity to talk individually to several board members and find out a lot about them. In the end, I put all the pieces together and got a clear picture of what was going on here.

Now I knew the board objectives and why they were not interested in my already proven innovation that could almost immediately solve the Medicare problems they had. The board objectives were different—they had focused on the $2 million fund they were now in charge of. Each of them kept receiving a huge salary from this fund every month.

The board wanted to stay on pretending they were "solving problem"—until they transferred all the money from the fund into their pockets in the form of their huge salaries. That was the board's major objective.

And here I was, wanting to short circuit their looting of the $2 million fund. I had promised to turn this health care company into the black within several weeks, not in many months, as they were planning. That was why to the board, I was "persona non grata" and their great antagonist.

In the meantime, while I had been on the 1st floor in the accounts receivable department, familiarizing myself with their problems, the board went after my new friend, an accountant. They educated him about their major objective, telling him that he made an error and had brought them the wrong person. If I solved the problem in a few weeks, their huge salaries would be stopped, and how was he, the accountant, now their new CFO, going to maintain his new life style and continue driving his new black Mercedes?

Driving back to San Francisco, we barely talked; we both understood what was going on and our respective roles. After that, I never heard from him again.

He had a copy of my Medicare reimbursement innovation blue print, and I assumed that after they looted all of the $2 million fund, only then would they "solve" the health care company problem. They would do so by using my innovation blueprint.

Dramatic Changes Were Everywhere

Why did no one want to hire me? The reason was simple. I was living in the past, assuming that no dramatic changes had taken place around me and that made me unemployable in 1998. I was wrong.

The world had changed. To learn about the outside changes and adjust accordingly to them, I started "looking through the window." Soon I discovered what was going on around me that I had been oblivious to before.

When I opened the quarterly financial statement of my IRA from my investment company, I could not believe what I saw: my lifetime retirement savings in the IRA was almost gone. Now I was on full alert, paying attention to life around me.

I went to Bank of America and when I could not find a slip to make a withdrawal, I asked a cashier where the slips were. She stated that now there were no more "free slips." Instead, customers must pay for slips. I was furious. Why?

Soon the local TV news answered my question. A president of Bank of America "...received $46 million salary." I connected the dots. That was why there were no more free withdrawal slips in the bank; customers were being milked for pennies so the crook could get an outrageous $46 million salary.

The evening local news started broadcasting a new trend, housing overbidding. One episode showed a senior couple, living somewhere in Silicon Valley, who were trembling from pleasant shock in front of a camera. Why?

Their old single-family house was for sale for several years, with an asking price of $190,000. They got not one offer, ever. Now, out of the blue, they were unexpectedly were swamped with 5–6 buyers competing for their old abbot.

When the competitive bidding stopped, it was revealed that the highest bidder bought their house for over $430,000. That is why the seniors were trembling from a happy surprise, as if they had won a big lottery.

What was going on? Some kind of fantasy adventures or scams? How and why was the annual salary of bank presidents, that were $40,000–$80,000 before, now magically raised into the stratosphere to $46 million; here millions of dollars replaced thousands. Why?

The reason was that President Bill Clinton's administration "relaxed" civil and criminal financial laws and Wall Street and their associates went amok inventing many scams.

One classic example of such scams was that perpetrated by "Arthur Andersen Consulting." Before 1996, it was an accounting consulting business for decades in the USA, and was considered to be one of the best international companies.

But, after 1996–1997, this consulting company changed 180 degrees and became a scam consulting company. How?

In order for the "dot-com" scam companies to sell their inflated stocks with nonexistent incomes and profit, they needed to partner with a reputable accounting consulting company. Consultants who would "cook" the "dot-com" companies' books by projecting their imaginary incomes and profits.

So, Arthur Anderson changed from a reputable consulting company into a scam and fraudulent consultancy overnight and started cooking books for "dot-com" companies for huge fees. For that, the executives at Arthur Anderson Consultants fired or laid off all of their employees who did not understand their overnight transformation into a scam company. During this time, I also applied to Arthur Anderson, sending them the record of my innovations, but I never received an answer from them.

Following their involvement in the collapse of Enron, later Arthur Anderson scammers were criminally prosecuted, the company went bankrupt, and was dissolved.[1]

Donald Trump—Life Without Opportunity

I was not the only one who in 1998 entered the period of "no opportunity" in my career. A classic example was Donald Trump, a "real estate genius" who also experienced a period of lack of opportunity in his real estate business between 1988–1996.

Life before 1996 for Donald Trump was not a rose garden; it was a nightmare. During this time, no one, not even the poorest person in the USA, wanted to trade places with him. He was bankrupt and owed $1–$2 billion in debt to many banks. No one was buying his old real estate. The media had a field day making fun of him and his misfortune.

There was constant news about his meetings with banker-creditors, where the major agenda of the day was "What should we do with Donald? Put him in the slammer or let him run the streets as a free man?"

News cameras even followed Mr. Trump on his Wal-Mart trips, now his favorite store, where he was buying everyday items made in China. Every night, jokes mocking him were on every late night entertainment show. There was no shortage of news about "The Donald." He was producing spicy entertainment fodder by going through his divorce with Ivana and his antics with his girlfriend Marla Maples.

Some Classic Examples of No Opportunity for Women

1. American women had no equal opportunity with men in employment and education until 1964, when the Civil Rights Act law was created. To enforce this law the Equal Employment Opportunity Committee, EEOC, was established in 1965. Even after the passage of the law, women experienced huge resistance from men for the next decades.

Women started entering colleges and, after graduating, still had to "prove" that they could perform the same jobs as men. Today, or 30–40 years later, 60% of American women graduated from colleges versus 40% of men, more women are employed than men, and women are more financially savvy than men. What a miracle American women have achieved in such sort time when they were given opportunity!

2. Russian women in 1918, after the November 1917 Revolution, were given an equal opportunity with men. With an opportunity, they made immense progress, and

by the 1960s, more than 75% of women were graduating with college degrees versus 25% of men. As for the fields of medicine and teaching, over 90% were women.

3. For Saudi Arabian women, even today, there is no equal opportunity. There, women are regarded as second-class citizens and are not allowed to enter university. Only recently in 2011, was the 1st university opened for women. But, when they graduate, there will be no jobs for them; no one is going to hire them. Here, ability is nothing without the opportunity.

△ △ △

THE MORAL OF THE STORY

It is simple: "Ability is nothing without opportunity." In my personal example with the opportunity, my skills and creativity bloomed; without opportunity, I produced nothing.

For the Donald Trump example, the same law of life applied. Before, he marketed himself as a real estate "genius" during the period when the real estate market was booming.

He was able to sell his real estate at inflated prices and made a lot of profit. Then times changed, the real estate boom stopped, housing went into the dead zone period (1986–1996), and Donald Trump went bankrupt. He was $1–$2 billion in debt. His real estate "genius" did not work during the real estate dead zone period. Mr. Trump had no opportunity to sell his real estate at inflated prices.

Before American women had no equal opportunity with men until the Civil Rights Act of 1964, that gave them equal opportunity rights. Today, or 30–40 years later, American women outperform men; 60% of them graduate from college, more women are employed, and women are more financially savvy than men.

Once the equal opportunity was given to American women, in just 30-40 years they outperformed their male counterparts and left them far behind.

Today Saudi Arabian women have no equal opportunity to men. A Saudi Arabian woman is just merchandize that can be bought and sold; she is not allowed to leave her home without a male relative escort, to drive a car, talk on a phone, and she must cover her body from head-to-toe, etc.

At the same time, women in Iran today are given an equal opportunity with men. And 60%

of Iranian women are graduating from colleges versus 40% of Iranian men.

When a person is given the opportunity, the sky is the only limit to his or her abilities, contributions, and achievements, as the above facts show. Without the opportunity a person is nothing.

---

[1] Enron was a company that sold natural gas and other energy-related products and investments. The company grew rapidly beginning in the early 1990s, when the USA Congress approved legislation deregulating the sale of natural gas. The company's stock price peaked in mid-2000 at nearly $100.00 per share. However, it came to light that $100 billion of revenue was in fact the result of accounting fraud. Arthur Anderson was directly involved in the scam and helped Enron cook their books. Ultimately, the stock's price fell to $1.00 per share.

SHORT STORY

Why Is Engineering the Most Prestigious Profession in the World, Except in the USA?

A Person Is a Product of Time, Place, and Circumstances

△ △ △

Recently there was some news on major national TV channels. Some American news correspondents recently traveled to major foreign countries to interview some high school students asking them: "What do you want to be?" Their uniform answers were: "I want to be an engineer."

Back in the USA, the correspondents put the same question to American high school students. Their answers were: "I want to be famous" and "I want to be rich." Why are there such huge discrepancies between 16–18 year old students in the USA and the rest of the world?

What Is Engineering? Who Are Engineers? What Do They Do?

What is engineering? A simple definition and answer comes from an engineer: everything around you that is man-made and not made by nature is—engineering, and is designed by engineers.

Engineers have designed innovations that have solved national problems, constructed and designed things (from bridges to computers), improved the quality of life for citizens, created national wealth, and contributed to the development of civilization.

Wikipedia gives a theoretical definition of an engineer: "An engineer is a professional practitioner of engineering, concerned with applying scientific knowledge, mathematics, and ingenuity to develop solutions for technical, societal, and commercial problems. Engineers design materials, structures, and systems while considering the limitations imposed by practicality, regulation, safety and cost."

The engineering profession is based on hard sciences where formulas are used to find solutions to various problems.

On the other hand, service industry professionals and all other jobs are arts, where no formulas are used, only personal common sense, imagination and opinion. Engineers see the world in 2 dimensions only: white or black; right or wrong.

That is, for every problem there are only 2 potential answers, or solutions: correct or wrong. Mistakes in engineering are unacceptable, as they are costly and intolerable. To illustrate this, let's consider some visual examples.

In the engineering profession: assume a bridge engineer made an error when calculating just one element of a bridge structure, say the deck. As soon as the bridge opened for traffic, the deck would start sagging, and soon the whole bridge structure would crumble and collapse. At the same time, engineers do not have communications, or PR (Public Relations) skills, since they do not need it; those skills are required by those who work in the service industry.

A Person Is a Product of Time, Place, and Circumstances

The service industry and most other jobs, such as lawyers, accountants, physicians, and business consultants, and many more, see the world in one dimension only—gray.

Here, in the gray area, there are no right or wrong answers. Instead, there are as many answers as there are service professionals. They need marketing skills to twist, manipulate, and present answers that a customer wants to hear, or what is the best for the service industry to increase their profit.

In the service industry, for every problem there are many answers. Each service professional may give a different solution to a problem or a different diagnosis depending on their expertise, creativity, and personal objectives.

For example, if a patient went to 5 different physicians complaining that he had swelling and needle pains in his hands, he may get 5 different diagnoses: rheumatoid arthritis, neuroma, arthritis, fibromyalgia, or peripheral neuropathy.

People are fascinated by engineering technology and use it everyday. They work and live in reinforced concrete buildings; use computers at work and at home to get information and simplify their business and personal life; drive fast cars using bridges, tunnels and roads; live in homes that have indoor plumbing; use electricity generated by dams and nuclear plants and watch TV channels brought by satellites; and are calling across the globe.

People use internet to retrieve information and communicate with others; fly on airplanes and use ships to go anywhere they want; they go to hospitals and medical centers equipped with medical technology; eat, drink, and wear garments produced and made in factories.

How Engineers Contributed to the Development of Civilization

Starting in the Ancient Era, engineers created many great engineering wonders and left them as a gift to future civilizations: pyramids, buildings, and towers, including the 7 Wonders of the World.

Consider their enormous scale when they had no other main resources available to them, except human capital. Egyptians constructed pyramids 4,600 years ago, Greeks built the Acropolis and Parthenon, and the Romans devised aqueducts and the Coliseum.

Other ancient projects include the hanging Gardens of Babylon, Machu Picchu, the pyramids of the Mayan, the Incan and Aztec Empires, the Taj Mahal in India, the Great Wall of China, and many, many more stand as testaments to the ingenuity, skills, and knowledge of the ancient civil engineers.

Their minds were so advanced and resourceful that thousands of years later, even today, no one can unlock the secrets of the past. How in their time, with limited technical resources except human capital, were they able to complete such engineering wonders and with such precision?

Those nations did not live selfish lives and waste all their national resources on themselves. They had noble leaders who channeled the genius of their people to build national wealth—advanced engineering marvels and icons of civilization. They built monuments for current generations, new wealth for future generations, and free gifts to civilization.

More recent great engineering projects include the Suez Canal in Egypt; Trans-Siberian Railway in Russia, Moscow subway in Russia; Golden Gate Bridge in San Francisco, Empire State Building in New York City, the Hoover Dam in Arizona, in the USA; the Aswan High Dam in Egypt; the Eiffel Tower in Paris and many, many more.

More engineering innovations include the first telephone in 1876; the 1st mechanical computer in 1890; the first electronic computers in 1943; the first ocean steamship in 1858; the first atomic weapon, the Manhattan project in 1943 (making the atomic bomb); the first jet engine in 1943; the first satellite, Sputnik in 1957; the first moon landing in 1969 and many more.

Earlier civilizations invented hard sciences by using common sense and observations of their everyday life and the world around them.

Arabs and Muslims developed algebra. Babylonians observed the sky and developed a calendar around 500

BC. Nicolaus Copernicus, a Polish astronomer, regularly observed the sky and in 1514 challenged the common belief which maintained that the Earth was the center of the universe. He proved that all planets, including Earth, moved in orbits around the sun. Isaac Newton (1642–1727), an English scientist, developed 3 laws of motion, the law of gravity, and the foundation for classical mathematics.

How Engineering Transformed Some Countries into Technological Powerhouses in the 20th Century? Russia, the Soviet Union, 1917–1991

The 700-year-old Russian empire under autocratic rulers Tsars (Emperors) was backward, far behind the industrial and progressive Europe. Russian nobility wanted to make Russia industrial and progressive; the Tsar was holding Russia back.

In November 1917, under the leadership of Vladimir Ilyich Lenin, they overthrew the Tsar regime and replaced it with the Socialist regime where workers and peasants were in charge.

The newly formed USSR (the Union Soviet Socialist Republics), or the Soviet Union, underwent massive engineering industrialization. Equal opportunity for all and mass education with an emphasis on engineering resulted in the building of hundreds of thousands of plants, military, and civilian industry.

A Person Is a Product of Time, Place, and Circumstances

The results were breathtaking. In less than 20 years, backward Imperial Russia was transformed into a strong, technologically developed power. It defeated Hitler during World War II (1941–1945).

But the country was destroyed and leveled by 3 years of war on Russian soil and 26.6 million people were killed, almost all men between the ages of 18 to 50. During 1945–1965, the country was rebuilt. In 1957, it shocked the world when it sent Sputnik into orbit. The world did not expect such technology to be developed for many generations.

After World War II, the Soviet Union became a world superpower, all thanks to engineering. Engineering was the most prestigious profession in the country. All Soviet Presidents and Politburo members were engineers. Why?

Engineers knew how to solve the country's problems, create national wealth, make the country's military strong and improve the quality of life of the population, and they know how to develop civilization.

The USA, 1930–Today

In the 1930s, the USA was in the Great Depression, unemployment was high, poverty, and long soup lines. It was a backward agricultural country, isolated by 2 ocean, and did not want to be involved in world and European affairs. There was no future or way out of the Great Depression. Then World War II started. Hitler took all of

Europe in just 3 months and on June 22, 1941, he invaded the Soviet Union. On December 17, 1941, the Japanese bombed Pearl Harbor. Those 2 events changed the USA.

Unemployed Americans went to work in factories to produce arms, equipment, and supplies for the wars and volunteered for the army. Joseph Stalin, the President of the Soviet Union, during 3 years of World War II on Russian soil asked the USA and Britain many times to open the 2nd front and stop the Russian bleeding. They refused stating that they were too weak to fight Hitler.

Only later, in June 1944, after the Soviet Army liberated the Soviet Union and Europe and was marching on Berlin, the USA and Britain, afraid that now the Soviet Union may take all Europe under its Empire, they decided to open the 2nd front.

In June 1944, they entered World War II and launched the Normandy Landing on the beaches of France. In May 1945, the Soviet Army took Berlin and on May 9, 1945, World War II ended.

After the war, tens of thousands of German engineers, afraid of Russian prosecution, escaped to the USA. Also, thousands of European engineers left war-devastated Europe and came to the USA. In the USA, they developed military, space, and civilian industries and transformed the USA from a backward agricultural separatist country into a world superpower.

A Person Is a Product of Time, Place, and Circumstances

In 1979, the USA celebrated the 10-year anniversary of landing man on the moon. On TV, they assembled approximately 40 engineers responsible for this program; all of them were Germans. Look at America's Silicon Valley today; the majority of the engineers are foreigners. If tomorrow they all left, the USA would become a less developing country.

Japan, 1950-1980, Was Transformed Into an Industrial Nation and #2 Economy in the World

In 1945, militant Japan surrendered to the Allied Powers. Defeated, Japan was put under international control, and no military was allowed. Instead, the USA took over responsibility to defend Japan. How did Japan, in such a short time (1950–1970), transform into the #2 industrialized nations in the world?

There were several factors responsible for Japan's rapid industrial development. Japan's resources that would usually be wasted on military were put into the civilian industry. The military industry was quickly re-engineered into the civilian industry after 1945.

Another factor, was the Japanese government's clever adoption of a wise *Law of life* in the trilogy "do not reinvent the wheel," instead "look through the window" to see what the outside world had invented already. Japan implemented the best parts from both systems into its economy—it had a socialist planning economy and a capitalist market economy.

The Japanese took outside inventions and improved, tweaked, and adopted them to fit their needs. From the Soviet Union, it took its educational system, labor laws, and government strategic planning.

For example, engineering is the most prestigious profession in Japan; they graduate 70,000 engineers per year, and only 1,000 lawyers, according to national needs, not wants.

Japan also took inventions in technology from the USA and Western Europe. They took foreign inventions apart and reversed engineered them; they became innovations as per Japanese and international needs. For example, they took parts from American and European cars, improved their quality, performance, and lowered their gasoline consumption.

They put improved parts into Japanese cars and exported these Japanese cars to the USA, Europe, and across the world. Japanese cars became the most reliable and inexpensive with low gasoline consumption.

The Japanese used strategic planning to plan their technological production and development based on outside factors, such as the price of gas for cars. Gas was going up, not down, so earlier in the 1970s they began producing smaller cars with high mileage per gallon.

At the same time, American automobile companies were using consumer surveys to find out what types of cars they should produce (actually cars were assembled, not produced). For example, at the beginning of the 1970s, Chrysler conducted consumer surveys asking if Americans still liked big Chrysler cars; the answer was yes.

Then, during the 1973–1974 Oil Embargo, the OPEC countries cut production of oil and quadrupled the price for a barrel of oil. The price of oil went up from $3 per barrel to $12. American consumers turned their attitude 180 degrees, from buying big Chrysler cars with 9–11 miles per gallon, to much smaller Japanese cars, like a Nissan or Toyota with a 20 miles per gallon fuel economy.

Today China Overtook the USA and Become the #1 Economy in the World

After the Soviet Union disintegrated in 1991, China changed from a socialist planning economy to a capitalist market economy. The socialist planning economy includes living below your means and planning production according to the needs of the population, not its wants. Capitalist market economy embraces the idea of "expansion in all directions without restrictions" and the market will correct itself.

Factors responsible for China's rapid growth include 600,000 engineering graduates annually. China's President is an engineer, as are members of the Central Committee of the Communist Party. They know how to solve the country problems and create national wealth, and how to design engineering inventions and innovations. Plus, they are using strategic planning from a socialist economy.

Why Are Americans Fascinated with Technology but Do Not Want to Become Engineers to Design Technology?

The American population is fascinated with technology, constantly on buying sprees for the latest technology and gadgets. Very few Americans want to become engineers to create the technology they are so fond of and are buying continually.

What is engineering? Everything around you that is made by man and not by nature—is engineering. Engineering is a difficult, responsible, and accountable profession. Everything that engineers design is on display; mistakes are not acceptable.

Engineers do not have communication and PR (Public Relations) skills to market and promote the engineering profession in the USA. They do not have a formidable association, as for example American physicians have in a form of the AMA (American Medical Association) that spends billions of dollars marketing and promoting the physician profession in the USA.

American high school children do not want to go to engineering colleges; they look on the internet and see that engineering colleges are the most difficult colleges, and require a lot of time to study, leaving no time left to party.

When engineers' salaries in the USA are low compared to physicians and lawyers, but their level of responsibility and accountability is large, and all their work is seen and on display for all to see. Engineers create national wealth, new jobs, and new industries.

△ △ △

THE MORAL OF THE STORY

What is engineering? Everything around you that is man-made and not by nature is—engineering. History is full of examples that, starting from the Ancient civilization, civil engineers created monumental projects as a symbol of national wealth.

Those nations did not live selfish, indulgent lives; instead, they sacrificed so their nations would survive and prosper. They channel the genius of their people into monumental projects that, in turn, created national wealth and contributed to the development of civilization.

Examples of ancient engineering marvels include the pyramids of Egypt, the Acropolis and Parthenon in Greece, the Roman aqueducts and Coliseum, Machu Picchu, the Taj Mahal in India, the Great Wall of China.

More recent great engineering projects are the Suez Canal, Aswan High Dam in Egypt; Trans-Siberian Railway in Russia, Moscow subway; Golden Gate Bridge in San Francisco, Empire State Building in New York City, Hoover Dam in Arizona, USA; Eiffel Tower in Paris, and many more.

Lets imagine for a moment if the USA President was an engineer. What a country the USA could become! He would solve all the USA's problems.

There would be no national debts over $19 trillions. An Engineer-President could never remunerate his big donors with $800 billon annual military expenses adding this debt each year to the already unsustainable national debt, and on the backs of the ordinary Americans.

He would not send American young men to die abroad in faraway countries to ignite political disturbances that will tear countries apart, killing innocent people just so the big American corporations, banks, and Wall Street get rich quick from the wars.

Instead, the Engineer-President would create national wealth and tens of millions of jobs, improve the quality of life of every citizen, would channel the genius and creativity of the American people into monumental projects and leave those monuments to present, and future generations and as a free gift to civilization.

What monuments is the present American generation leaving after itself? In the past 20 years, no national wealth was built, the same time oil and raw resources have depleted, and overpopulation and carbon monoxide produced an ecological holocaust that threaten the survival of the present civilization.

SHORT STORY

What Is National Wealth?
How National Wealth Created?
Who Creates National Wealth?

A Person Is a Product of Time, Place, and Circumstances

△ △ △

How and why do some countries become great and contribute to the development of civilization? They channeled the creativity, genius, and knowledge of their people into building engineering projects as monuments for themselves and left this national wealth for future generations, such as the Egyptians, Greeks, Romans, and many more.

In the last 20 years, no national wealth was created in the USA; this was the reason for high unemployment and increasingly long economic recessions.

Why is the creation of national wealth so important? Building national wealth creates millions of jobs and improves the quality of people's lives of the present and future generations.

Even more, national wealth is a symbol of a people's generational genius, their creativity, skills, knowledge, and contribution to the development of their nation and civilization.

What national wealth is the USA building today as monuments after itself and is leaving for the future generations? None.

Rachel Maddox, an MSNBC news broadcaster, likes to broadcast a particular episode as an example of national wealth. Standing next to the Hoover Dam, she points out that "our parents and grandparents" created this marvel of engineering for us. And what we did or do today?

One wonders what genius, creativity, and achievement the 1930s generation must have had that could have designed and built such a magnificent monument—this national wealth—the dam, to satisfy national needs for many generations. The Hoover Dam is producing electricity for millions of people today, and has been since its construction.

What Is National Wealth?

Money as wealth is not listed here. Money has an intrinsic value; it is intangible and is difficult to qualify.

Real money (dollars) changed hands in the last 20 years from Main Street (middle class) pensions, IRAs, and savings to Wall Street crooks who overnight became millionaires, 6.4 million of them, and they are holding that money in Switzerland's banks and in offshore accounts. Consider these 4 types of national wealth:

1. Wealth created by nature: land, ocean, rivers, trees, mountains, wild animals, fish, and water. Raw natural resources: oil, gas, iron, coal, copper, cobalt, nickel, silicon, gold, and silver.

2. Wealth created by men: everything around you made by men and not by nature: superstructures, infrastructures, factories, plants, buildings, modern cities, bridges, roads, products, machinery, instruments,

means of transportation, power lines, water and sewer systems, dams, computers, household appliances, medical technology, and many more.

3. People's character traits: stoic, ingenious, resilient, nationalistic, work ethic, patriotic, sophisticated, positive thinking, having dignity and honor.
4. Noble president and honest government: noble and nationalistic, intellectual, not corrupt and selfish.

A noble president is a visionary, who puts the country's needs above his personal ones, who transforms the country into a progressive and technologically competitive nation, creates a positive environment for innovations to improve the quality of people's lives, has dignity and honor, and enforces equality, rules, and regulations against scams and financial crimes that bankrupt the nation and people.

The president and the federal government are responsible for the well-being of all citizens and the security and survival of the nation, especially in today's uncertain and unstable world. This requires having laws and regulations that prohibit the powerful who are the crooks and thieves from conducting financial scams and robbing and looting to make the majority of the people poor.

History is full of examples of how, in the past, some American presidents created national wealth and contributed to the development of the USA. How noble President Franklin D. Roosevelt, FDR, during the 1930s

Depression saved the USA from economic crisis and transformed it from an agricultural separatist country that did not want to be involved in international affairs into a league of nations. When World War II started, FDR declared: "There will be no war millionaires."

How John F. Kennedy, JFK, after Sputnik, developed the USA space program to compete with the Soviet Union that later landed a man on the moon and these space technology innovations spilled into the civilian sectors and created a consumer industry with many products.

How President Dwight Eisenhower, when fighting in Europe during World War II, having seen European bridges and roads, then return home and transformed the USA's dirty roads into modern roads, and the interstate highway system.

How to Create National Wealth?

To understand how to create national wealth, let's take here some simple and familiar examples and use a simple skill—visualization.

Example #1: Designing and Building a Bridge

The USA federal government had a project to satisfy the population's needs. It needed to build a 10-span bridge with 4 ramps, I-95, in downtown Baltimore over the Patapsco River. A bid was announced for this bridge. Many engineering companies competed for the bid; one company won and received, say $4 million from the federal government to design this bridge.

To design this bridge, the company hired a new staff of engineers, draftsmen, technical, supporting, and administrative personnel; in total 45 people.

One structural engineer from the staff was chosen to design this bridge, alone, and was paid a salary say of $87,000 per year with no bonuses or pension. The engineer designed this bridge, blueprints of drawings, and calculations in 12 months, approximately.

Next, a bid for the bridge construction was announced. Here the bridge drawings and calculations were divided into many projects ready for bids from many contractors, subcontractors, and engineering companies, big and small. In the end, 50–60 companies won bids, and the construction of the bridge started.

Many thousands of new people were hired: construction workers, supervisors, foremen, managers, engineers, technicians, and administrators.

The bridge designers and building companies, except for a small profit, did not become millionaires, nor did they get rich quick. The work was hard, dangerous, challenging and stressful; all the people who were involved in the bridge design and construction made a huge contribution to the nation. They gave more to the nation and took back for themselves very little, just small salaries.

After 3 years, the bridge construction was over, say the $3–$5 billion bridge was finished and become the national wealth—it will serve the transportation needs of the population for generations.

In short, the original investment, called a seed, $87,000, that was paid to the bridge design engineer, created many thousands of new jobs and produced a $3–$5 billion bridge—the national wealth for generations.

That is how national wealth was created!

Example #2: Planting an Orange Tree

Let's take another simpler analogy. A farmer bought 2–3 dry orange seeds for 50 cents. He then planted these seeds to grow an orange tree. The tree grew and 5–6 years later, matured and began bearing $200–$300 of oranges per season, a new revenue. The farmer hired a worker to pick the oranges and then sold the oranges to supermarkets and food processors to make orange juice.

To summarize: originally, 2–3 orange seeds bought for 50 cents grew and began producing $200–$300 in revenue from oranges each season and created new jobs. In the process, no one got rich quick, or became a millionaire.

The farmer, an orange picker, the supermarkets, and other workers worked hard for small salaries, or minimum wages; they gave more to society and took back for themselves very little. Oranges satisfy national needs; it is a food for the population. This orange tree became the national wealth for many generations, as it feeds the population.

That is how national wealth was created!

Who Creates National Wealth?

Who creates national wealth? Engineers do. Remember how civilizations were developed and flourished? From building monumental civil engineering projects.

Egyptians: pyramids; Greeks: the Acropolis and Parthenon; the Romans: aqueducts and Coliseum; Machu Picchu; Taj Mahal in India; the Great Wall of China; the Suez Canal in Egypt; the Trans-Siberian Railway in Russia, Moscow subway; the Golden Gate Bridge in San Francisco, Empire State Building in New York City, the Hoover Dam in Arizona; High Dam in Aswan, Egypt; Eiffel Tower in Paris; telephone in 1876, computers, first atomic weapon, Manhattan project, first satellite, Sputnik in 1957, the first moon landing in 1969, and many, many more.

These monumental projects were possible due to their countries noble leaders who channeled the genius and intellect of their people to build advanced engineering marvels, new wealth for their countries, and gifts to civilization.

Engineers, inventors, innovators, entrepreneurs, and ordinary people put their creativity and genius into creating new ideas, inventions, and innovations.

To transform their ideas into physical things, they asked engineers to create innovations—to design a structure, a product, a software program, or a service. Engineers created innovations and transformed these innovations into blueprints (drawings and calculations). Then, from these blueprints various products and structures are built.

How many engineers became millionaires from building national wealth and from creating trillions of dollars worth of different structures and products? Not many, probably none. Engineers' contributions to a society and to the nation—are noble contributions—they give a lot to the nation and take back very little for themselves.

That is why engineering is the most prestigious profession in the world, except in the USA. Every high school student in the world dreams of becoming an engineer, and the brightest and most gifted apply to engineering colleges, except in the USA. Here high school students want to be famous, or rich.

Wall Street Does Not Create Any National Wealth. Instead It Created 6.4 Million New Millionaires by Robbing Americans and the World

The noble contribution of engineers does not apply to Wall Street. Wall Street does not create any national wealth. In the last 20 years, no national wealth was created in the USA, but at the same time 6.4 million Wall Street crooks became new millionaires.

How? From robbing the American people, the USA Treasury, and the world using their financial scams: "dot-com," "subprime mortgages," and the banks' "zero interest rates," and many more. Wall Street destroyed the American middle class and as a result, 1 in 2 Americans today is living in poverty or near the poverty line.

Wall Street robbed the American people and the world, pushed the USA economy into Financial Crisis in September 2008 and then asked the USA government to bail them out. The USA government did bail out their big donors—Wall Street—with over $700 billion.

The USA is run by very clever criminals. The Federal Reserve with its scam of "0% interest rates" forced the population to give their money to the banks for free. They received no interest on their money, all so the bank's crooks could give them loans at 4%–25% interest.

With this scam, bankers made over $3 trillion. They are hoarding this money to pay themselves billions in salaries and bonuses.

Some classic examples from Wall Street:

1). Mr. Henry Paulson, the Former Secretary of the Treasury, worked for the guru of Wall Street, Goldman Sachs. There he accumulated $130–$140 million in personal wealth. He created no national wealth; instead he made his wealth from Wall Street scams.

2). Mr. Bill Gates (Microsoft) has $70–$80 billion net personal wealth that he does not need. How did he get such enormous wealth? From greed.

He sold his Microsoft software at the inflated prices of $300–$400 apiece to the minimum wage workers whose earnings are $5–$7 per hour. His greed is pitiful, his company does not have even a free 800 number to call for technical support.

To get to Mr. Gates' technical support, a software buyer must pay for his long distance telephone calls. At the same time, Mr. Gates likes to parade on TV advertising his charity to Africa. Mr. Gates, charity starts at home. Stop robbing your fellow American citizens. Stop selling them software at inflated prices that they cannot afford. Mr. Gates gave 1%–5% to society, but took for himself the lion share of 95%–99% in profits.

△ △ △

THE MORAL OF THE STORY

What is national wealth? Everything around you that is man-made and not created by nature—is engineering or national wealth. Who creates national wealth? Engineers, inventors, innovators, entrepreneurs, and ordinary people.

How does one create national wealth? National wealth can only be created under the leadership of a noble president and honest government.

In the last 20 years, the USA had no noble president and no national wealth was created. In the past, the USA had a noble President, Franklin D. Roosevelt. Even he was a rich man, but he put his country and his people above himself and did not focus on enriching himself. When World War II started, he declared: "There will be no war millionaires." He had a measure of dignity and honor.

The USA needs a noble president, not greedy and corrupt politicians whose doctrine is: "New world disorder." They keep starting new wars across the world so big donors—Wall Street, big companies, banks, and the military industry—get rich quick from looting the USA Treasury to pay for their war campaigns and put their wars expenses—over $19 trillion as unsustainable ticking national debts and war's suffering on the shoulders of the American people.

Engineering must become the most prestigious profession in the USA, as it is in the rest of the world. Engineers must solve the economy's problems, create national wealth, and create millions of new jobs. They must become the policymakers and government advisors. Today, economists are the government advisors. How many economists have created national wealth and new jobs? None.

Do you know that there are thousands of noble Americans who would give their lives to become a USA president, senators, and congressmen so they could serve this country with dignity and honor? They would create national wealth and millions of new jobs that would improve the quality of American lives and pull the USA from the grips of the Financial Crisis.

SHORT STORY

How Many Millionaires Are in the USA? What Types?

△ △ △

A millionaire, by dictionary definition, is a person whose net worth is equal to or above $1 million in a bank account or in a savings account. In old Europe until the 18th century, a millionaire status belonged to only one special elite class, the nobility and royalty. To become a millionaire in old Europe one had to be born into that class.

Not in America. The new country has changed the old European tradition and become an inspiration and attraction for all emigrants from the Old World.

To become a millionaire was everyone's dream—the American dream. A new concept of the American millionaire has developed, where everyone can become a millionaire in the USA in a traditional way "from rags to riches" i.e., through thrift, creativity, innovation, entrepreneurship, hard work, frugality, self-sacrifice, dignity, and honor.

Millionaires created national wealth, new industries, built the nation and created new jobs for the population. This American concept on how to become a millionaire the traditional way was practiced for over 200 years, until the 1990s.

All that has changed severely. Since the mid-1990s, the traditional way of creating an American millionaire has been abandoned and replaced by Wall Street scams and schemes to "get rich quick from thin air" by robbing and looting the middle class of their hard earned money, the USA government, the Treasury, and the world.

Today, no longer are entrepreneurial traits of creativity, innovation, hard work, persistence, dignity, and honor required or needed.

How Many Millionaires Are in the USA?

The total number of American millionaires created in 3 time periods is 10 million:[1]

	1st period	2nd period	3rd period
Years:	1776–1991	1991–2000	2000–2006
Millionaires:	3.6 million	3.6 million	2.8 million

The 1st period: 1776-1995

The 1st period, 1776–1991, or over 200 years: approximately 3.6 million traditional American millionaires were created.

During the first 200 years of American history, before 1991, to become a traditional millionaire "from rags to riches" was an American dream that was difficult and took a lifetime. The majority of millionaires were made during the Industrial Revolution in the 19th and 20th centuries when hundreds of thousands of inventions and innovations transformed America from a predominately rural and agricultural country into a technologically advanced superpower, creating a huge new working middle class, the consumers.

Since the beginning, America went through many technological revolutions whose innovations and inventions transformed the country and built national wealth: superstructures, infrastructures, industrial revolutions, assembly lines, transportation, factories, roads, bridges, railroads, oil refineries, banking, military and civilian industries, and space race programs. These innovations brought value to the society and improved the quality of American's lives.

Technological revolutions during the first 200 years created many traditional American millionaires: Rockefeller, Du Pont, Gatsby, Carnegie, Vanderbilt, Henry Ford, Lafayette, Getty, Morgan, Cooke, Macy, Duke, Howard Hughes, and many more. By 1991, there were 3.6 million traditional millionaires in the USA and 96 billionaires.

At that time, among the CEOs, presidents and managers in corporations, organizations, and institutions very few, if any, received a million dollars in salaries. The requirements for them equated to the huge responsibility of producing quality products and services, having low turnovers and high productivity, and making profits. There were no million-dollar bonuses either.

Until 1996 Merrill Lynch's stockbrokers and financial advisors were canvassing door-to-door in middle-class neighborhoods, soliciting new investors to use their services. The same way as an *Encyclopedia Britannica* salesmen went door-to-door in the same neighborhood selling their encyclopedias.

Banks and the banking profession had low pay and dull, unexciting jobs, and bonuses were not in the banks' vocabulary. The least creative and ambitious people went to work for banks; their salaries were well below $100,000. During this period, the average American citizen's life was simple and predictable: hard work, responsibility, nationalism, dignity, and honor. It took a lifetime of hard work to save for retirement.

The 2nd Period: 1991-2000

The 2nd period, 1991–2000: 3.6 million Wall Street millionaires were created by the new crooks through their 1st scam, "dot-com."

All hell broke loose in the 1990s. Laws and regulations were crossed out, deleted, and diluted, as in the Wild West.

What was true during the first 200 years of American history was out the window, and scams and schemes one after another were, and continued to be manufactured, even today as I am writing this story. "Get rich quick from thin air" swept the USA as tornadoes and millions of Wall Street crooks started popping up overnight as new millionaires, robbing and looting the American population to satisfy their greed.

The target was a middle-class treasure chest with over $3 trillion inside it. By the mid-1990s, the middle class, or Main Street, by working hard all their lives, accumulated in their pensions, IRAs, and individual accounts over $3 trillion dollars. Wall Street had big eyes on those trillions of dollars, itching for how to rob the middle-class of their hard earned trillions. Soon they manufactured and launched their 1st scam, "dot-com," from 1995–2000.

To implement their 1st scam "dot-com" Wall Street—for example, the Lehman Brothers, Goldman Sachs, Merrill Lynch, Bear Stearns, and other scammers—created thousands of illusory IPOs (Initial Public Offerings) for companies called "dot-com" that had no income and no possibility of ever having one.

They then sent armies of "consultants" (remember the leader in scam accounting consulting Arthur Anderson?) to illusory "dot-com" companies and old-line companies (Enron, Global Crossing, Amazon.com, and many others) "to cook up their books." Wall Street sold shares of all those companies at inflated prices, up to $400/share, to middle class pensions, IRAs, and savings accounts.

In 2000, the Wall Street bubble burst, the stock market crashed and produced losers and winners.

The losers were the American middle class. They lost over $3 trillion in their pensions, IRAs, and in savings accounts.

The winners were Wall Street crooks. In just 5 years, 3.6 million of them became new millionaires from their "dot-com" scam. Also, during this period, 176 new billionaires were created. By 2000, there were 272 billionaires in the USA, or a 283% increase in 5 years, when only 96 traditional billionaires were created during the first 200 years in America.

What did the Wall Street new millionaire crooks do with their overnight fortunes? They went wild buying airplanes, boats, expensive cars, toys, and real estate from easy money.

They bought real estate in their own headquarters, New York City and rescued Donald Trump from his $1–$2 billion real estate bankruptcy. Once resurrected, or once the "dead cat bounced," Mr. Trump went on TV parading as usual misrepresenting himself as "a real estate genius" and not a snake oil salesmen, as Rosie O'Donnell categorized him.

The 3rd Period: 2000-2006

The 3rd period, 2000–2006: 2.8 million Wall Street millionaires were created by new crooks from the 2nd scam "subprime mortgages."

After the "dot-com" scam, the market crashed in 2000. The middle class lost all their money, and did not trust Wall Street any longer. The real money was gone.

What did Wall Street do next? They manufactured a 2nd scam, called "subprime mortgages." This time, the target was the low-income population, who had little money and even less ability to pay huge subprime mortgages. Wall Street sold them 3–5–10 times inflated subprime mortgages for single houses and condos.

Soon, new real estate owners could not pay their huge subprime mortgages and went into foreclosures and bankruptcy. And what did the Wall Street crooks do next? They diced and sliced these subprime mortgages and sold them by blocks at illusory prices to Europe and other sovereigns across the world.

The result was: from 2000–2006, or in just 6 years, 2.8 million Wall Street crooks became new millionaires from their 2nd scam "subprime mortgages," and Iceland, Greece, Spain, Portugal, Italy, and many more other countries, that bought those blocks of the Wall Street subprime mortgages nearly collapsed.

Also, during this 8-year period, 197 new billionaires were created. By 2008, there were 469 billionaires in the USA, or a 488% increase from 1991 (when it took over 200 years to create 96 traditional billionaires).

From Where Does Wall Street Continue Getting Money for Their Scams?

The salary of Americans has not grown in the last 20–25 years, but the number of new millionaires keeps growing.

It is a big discrepancy. Where do Americans keep getting money to finance all these scams and schemes of the new Wall Street millionaires? No mystery here.

The answer is simple—from the total personal debts of Americans that have grown exponentially, from approximately $4 trillion in 1991 to $17 trillion in 2014. Total personal debt levels of Americans have consistently risen over a 30-year period, 1961–1991.

However, the rate of debts has astronomically increased since 2000. Between 2000 and 2008, the amount of personal debts has doubled.

The 1st sign of consumer distress was seen in the housing volatility and expansion of subprime mortgage credit that emerged in 2000, which contributed to the overall rise in total personal debts. Housing foreclosures have skyrocketed since 2006, and bankruptcy filing quadrupled. The USA has had the highest rate of personal bankruptcy filing in the world since 2005.

The 2nd sign of consumer distress is the growth of credit card debt. It grew from $181 billion in 1991, to $525 billion in 2000, and to $1 trillion in 2014, or grew by 550% from 1991.

The 3rd sign of consumer distress is the growth of student loans from $200 billion in 2000 to $1.1 trillion in 2014. Since 2010, the $1.1 trillion of student loan debt surpassed consumer credit card debt.

Types of American Millionaires in American History. Before 1991 and After 1991

What are the different types of American millionaires? Money does not grow on trees. Wall Street cannot print money, only the Federal Reserve can.

So, from where did the new 6.4 Wall Street scammers and connivers get their fast money after 1991? What are the types of American millionaires?

I. Traditional American millionaires, before 1991; 1776–1991.

For the first 200 years in America, there was only one type of millionaire—traditional millionaires. It was an American dream to become a millionaire through hard work, creativity, innovations, sacrifices, dignity, and honor; and to create national wealth, build the country and create jobs for the population.

Traditional millionaires got their personal wealth by creating national wealth.

II. Wall Street scam millionaires and many other types that got their millions from only one source— American people and the USA Treasury.

In the last 20 years, the types of millionaires in the USA has significantly changed, from traditional millionaires into Wall Street fast-buck ones: CEOs, bankers, professional athletes, movie stars, politicians, lawyers, and physicians.

New millionaires got their wealth by robbing the American middle class, the USA government, the USA Treasury, and American taxpayers. To pay no taxes they hide their money in Swiss banks, as well as in Bermuda and the Cayman Islands. These millionaires create no national wealth. Today, there are several types of these millionaires, they are listed below.

- Wall Street scammers and schemers;
- Corporate;
- Banks;
- Entertainment and sports. Movie stars, TV shows, actors, and professional athletes are paid millions;
- Private and public colleges;
- Physicians and lawyers;
- Politician millionaires: Former presidents, former vice presidents, senators, congressmen, governors and states lawmakers;
- Accidental or lucky: Game show contestants, state lotteries, casino gamblers, and injury compensation.

III. Types of millionaires that got their wealth by robbing and looting the USA government:

- Military industry, DOD (Department of Defense);
- Private military contractors;
- NSA (National Security Administration);
- Private prison companies.

△ △ △
THE MORAL OF THE STORY

How many millionaires are in the USA? What types?

In the last 20 years, the American dream to become a traditional millionaire through hard work, entrepreneurship, frugality, dignity, honor, and design of innovations to create national wealth and improve the quality of peoples' lives is gone. The American middle class has all but disappeared.

The traditional American millionaires were replaced by scammers and schemers millionaires "get rich quick from thin air" mentality. Hard work, dignity, and honor were replaced by greed and shopping sprees to buy wants, not needs, and hide money offshore from the IRS.

The USA government in order to finance the big corporations, the military industry, and private contractors—their big political donors—is constantly engaging in wars on faraway continents and looking for new conflicts to start. "The new world disorder" is a doctrine of President Barack Obama.

Money does not grow on trees. New millionaires want real money, not paper or imaginary money. Where do new millionaires get money to implement their scams and schemes? By robbing and looting the American population, the USA government, and the American nation.

This has made the USA national debt skyrocket from "0" in 1995 to $19 trillion in 2014, and USA citizens' personal debt has increased from $4 trillion in 1991 to $17 trillion in 2014.

Today there are 10 million millionaires in the USA, whereas from 1776–1996, or over 200 years, 3.6 million real traditional American millionaires were created. They developed America from an agricultural nation into a world superpower, and created national wealth.

From 1991–2006 another type of 6.4 million new millionaires were created from Wall Street scams and schemes. Today, the number of new crooks-millionaires continues to grow as they keep inventing new scams and schemes.

They created no national wealth. Instead, they have robbed and looted American people, destroyed the middle class, and pushed the USA economy into a financial crisis.

---

[1] http://thewellnessrevolution.paulzanapilzer.com/millionairs.php

SHORT STORY

What Is Amok? Or, Housing Amok

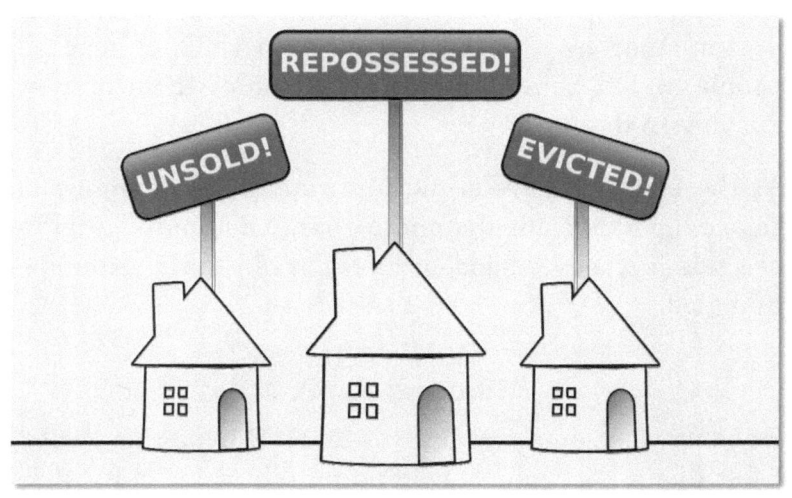

△ △ △

When I was young, I had read a dramatic book about a tropical climate disease called "Amok." I do no remember the author, but the story took place somewhere in Indonesia.

A man in his mid-20s, as if possessed by a demon, moved across the city with horrifying fury and frightening strength, crashing into and killing everybody and everything that stood in his path.

Terrified and to alert others, people quickly created noises by beating drums and anything else they could find around them to produce warning signals, and in terror they yelled and screamed "Amok! Amok!"

The amok man continued his insane bullet run, accompanied by warning signals from walls of shocked people he left behind and from all those whom he now encountered.

At the end of his life's journey, suddenly his supply of rage evaporated, his dynamite energy detonated, and in seconds his body exploded; he collapsed to the ground—and died.

Housing Amok

Housing went amok from 2003–2005. During this period, I felt like a shoe polisher standing idly next to my shoe

A Person Is a Product of Time, Place, and Circumstances

polish stand watching high speed trains, filled with thousands of excited home buyers whizzing by.

It seemed like the whole country went amok, trying to get rich quick from buying, selling, flipping, and renting houses and condos. At this time, everyone was talking about the housing boom. The housing environment was contagious, and excitement was in the air.

At that time, I was living in a huge apartment complex called "Sunset" in Florida which had 1,000 apartments. Just yesterday, "condo convertors" descended on our 20-year-old apartment complex, and they brought with them a team of loan bankers and appraisers.

On that day, my apartment complex was quickly sold to "condo convertors" from Miami at an average price of $15,000 for a 1-bedroom apartment and $20,000 for a 2-bedroom apartment.

The next day, the new owners of our apartment complex began calling themselves "the condo convertors" and re-named our old apartments into "condo conversions," and put all the apartments up for sale at the astronomical prices of $200,000 for a 1-bedroom apartment and $250,000 for a 2-bedroom apartment. Overnight, they increased the price for an average apartment 10-13 times!

We, the renters, received some flyers and contracts enticing us to buy our rented apartments, now re-named overnight as "condos," at such exorbitant prices. As for those renters who did not want to buy, and for prospective buyers from outside, the "condo convertors" designed an exciting marketing scheme.

To attract attention to their condo sales extravaganza, they created a festive atmosphere. Several loud speakers were installed at the entrance of now "the condo" complex and around the rental office that played popular songs.

Hard drinks and hot food were served all day into the evening at newly installed tables, and the mortgage bankers sat at kiosks offering their services.

A condo marketing team made up of strong, young men and former gang members, imported from Los Angeles for this occasion, was standing by to answer all the questions.

I did not fall to their temptations and would not buy a condo. Instead, I gave free lectures to anyone who was willing to listen, not to buy these apartments renamed into condos and warned them that it was a housing bubble running amok and a real estate scam. I gave them the facts.

One of them was the life span of apartments. Everything, I postulate, has a life span: computers are designed to last for 3 years, dishwashers for 5 years, cars for 10 years, reinforced concrete apartment buildings are designed for 25 years, commercial buildings for 37 years, and bridges for 43 years on average.

A Person Is a Product of Time, Place, and Circumstances

Even we humans have an average life span. We were designed to live for 45 years if we lived one century ago or are living now in Africa, and for about 70-85 years if living in Europe or the USA. Furthermore, I asked my listeners if they knew that when they bought a condo, a condo-seller must send them a certificate-statement by registered mail detailing how many structural years were left for that particular condo.

Don't believe me? Then go online to check Florida state law and find this particular law requirement for yourself. Florida law states that if the condo/apartment building, like mine in this case, that was 20 years old, that meant that it only had 5 years of structural life left in it (calculate: a new apartment building was designed for 25 years, minus the present condo age of 20 years old =5 years).

Therefore, a condo-seller certificate should state that there is only 5 years of structural life left in the condo you are buying. Knowing this fact, a prospective condo buyer should use common sense and make a simple decision—whether or not to pay the 10–13 times inflated price for the condo? In short, using this analogy, is a buyer willing to pay the same price for a 20-year-old Chevrolet as he would for a new car?

My listeners were speechless, when they heard me saying the above housing facts and common sense and kept repeating: "Why hasn't anyone ever told me this? It is so simple—why did I never think about it?" My reply was from *the Law of Life*: "Everyone wants you to be dumb, uninformed, and enveloped in a cloud of ignorance; that way, those who sell real estate will be able to sell you fool's gold as if it were the real deal."

Nothing lasts forever and so too was the housing amok. Soon, the housing amok exhausted itself, became unsustainable, and it popped, collapsed, and died in 2008. My "Sunset" complex had the same fate as all the other housing bubble running amok across the USA—it went bankrupt.

Condo owners, now new landlords, who came from all over the USA to get rich quick, bought the Sunset condos to rent out. They paid inflated prices for these condos with no down payment and took on "subprime mortgages."

Soon they faced the music; there were no tenants to rent the condos to and no money to pay the huge mortgages and condo fees. They went bankrupt and the 1,000 units in the "Sunset" complex were converted back into apartments. *Life in the Sunset apartment complex went on as if nothing ever happened!*

The housing amok repeated itself in 2011 with a new twist. Now 50% of the buyers were paying for overpriced old housing (in the majority of the cases) with cash. How long did this amok last? Not long—it was just a flash in the pan.

△ △ △
THE MORAL OF THE STORY

What is an amok? It is a tropical disease when a man (women do not have such a disease) suddenly explodes into a frenzy, running, charging violently and killing everyone on his path until he is exhausted and dies or is killed by others. An analogy to a man amok is the housing amok in 2003–2005 and again in 2011.

Many more amok are percolating today:

1) The world population is growing amok. Oil and raw resources are rapidly being consumed and exhausted. Climate change may lead to future ecological holocausts. Gambling and pervasive schemes to get-rich-quick flourish with minimum oversight and regulation and impoverishing the population quickly is amok.

2) The housing amok. It is produced by the real estate and mortgage scams; examples are 2003–

2005 and 2011–2014. Prices for old and new housing were going amok, regardless of the fact that a house, like a car, depreciates and does not appreciate.

To find the real price or depreciation for an old car—one can go to as authorities like Kelly Blue Book—and voila, find the precise depreciated value of a car.

Why do such websites not exist for housing? The answer is obvious—money and marketing. The real estate industry is the most secretive industry; they spend millions of dollars every year to market, program, and indoctrinate people into thinking that a house that is aging and deteriorating—"appreciates." And a single family house made from plywood is "the American dream."

SHORT STORY

Why Do Immigrants in the USA Speak with Foreign Accents?

△ △ △

"Why do you speak with a foreign accent?" I have heard this question numerous times. The person asking usually wants to know why I do not speak with an American accent. I had no answer to this "foreign accent" phenomenon.

To find the answer, I looked outside and began observing the world around me. I found many instances where very intelligent people tried to learn to speak with an American accent and failed. Why?

For example, for the famous Hollywood actor Arnold Schwarzenegger, it was crucial to speak with an American accent, yet he still speaks with a thick Austrian accent. He came to the USA at age 21, and later a Hollywood studio made a substantial afford in helping him to get rid of his foreign accent, or at least diminish it. Not much success, why?

For Henry Kissinger, the former Secretary of State who represented the USA across the world, but did not speak in an American accent. He was in the country for many decades and still speaks with a thick foreign accent, why?

Even for British journalists living in the USA for a long time, learning to speak with an American accent is very important for their career, as a substantial percent of the American population has difficulty in understanding their British accent. Regardless of the requirements and problems, they speak with their native British accent, why? Immigrants I have met all speak with a foreign accent, why?

Why do my children, who came to the USA together with me, do not speak with a foreign accent? Instead, they speak perfect American English. No one has ever thought they were not Americans and were not born here, why?

When I put all my observations and information together, then using logic and common sense, I noticed one red thread connects all of the immigrants—the age! The age was a major deciding factor in the "foreign accent" phenomenon. That was progress in my quest to unlock this mystery; it made sense. I was on the right track to discover an answer.

The next step was to find a critical age period, beyond what age a person could not learn an American accent. I began covering a much younger age cohort, young children of foreigners. I found that the critical age period was puberty, ages 12–13, when profound physiological changes take place in a child's young body. Hormonal changes transformed boys' soprano vocal cords into baritone voices and girls started budding breasts, preparing them for motherhood.

Now I learned 2 main factors were responsible for having a "foreign accent:" age and puberty; after puberty it was impossible for immigrants to change their foreign accents.

What body organs are responsible for speech was my next question. Active speech organs: lips and tongues. What active parts are involved in, for example, pronouncing consonant "th" to make sounds in the, they, their, than, there, cloth, bath?

This "th" consonant is a unique American pronunciation. When pronouncing "th", other types of active parts are added to the voice speech: the glottis (vocal cords) and larynx (voice box) of the throat. Puberty physiologically changes vocal cords in the throat and speaking from the back of the throat. That was the answer.

For the immigrants in the USA, in order not to speak with their "foreign accents," they must start speaking American English before puberty, that is, before a body physiologically changes from puberty to adolescence—a transitional stage "to grow up" took place.

After puberty, it is impossible to get rid of immigrants' "foreign accent." No one can change nature. That is why immigrants' children who came with their parents to the USA before their puberty virtually eliminated any "foreign accent" and have no language disparity with the American children they grew up with.

The majority of foreign languages are spoken with tongues and lips; the glottis and larynx are not very active speech organs. Brits speak British English, as all Europeans with actively involved lips and tongues.

Brits, I think, only passively involve their glottis and larynx to pronounce some consonants, for example: "th". That is why British immigrants, or journalists living in the USA for a long time, still speak with their British accent.

Now I was armed with my hypothesis as to why I, and millions of other immigrants who had been living in the USA for a while, still spoke with a "foreign accent."

△ △ △

THE MORAL OF THE STORY

Why do immigrants in the USA speak with a "foreign accent" even when they have been living here for a while? For the last 2 decades, I kept answering this question, using my hypothesis of "foreign accent" to anyone who was willing to listen.

All immigrants speak their native languages with lips and tongues only; the glottis and larynx are passive speech organs. When Americans, on another side, do not speak English with their lips.

Instead, their speech actively involve the glottis (vocal cords) and larynx (the vocal box).

Physical changes of the body occur during puberty, a critical period for speaking with an American accent. If immigrants started learning American English after puberty, they could never speak with an American accent; no one can change nature.

No one ever challenged or disagreed with me. To them, my hypothesis about "foreign accent" was based on common sense and observations of other immigrants around me. They were glad to learn about it.

Here, I am encouraging my readers, after reading this story, to challenge my hypothesis of "foreign accents" and in doing so generate more information and knowledge about this phenomenon.

ACKNOWLEDGEMENTS

△ △ △

Many people directly or indirectly make many contributions to my books. But the biggest contributors, who made fundamental changes and altered the directions of my writing, were 2 men.

Dr. Samuel Oliner, who, after learning about my writing of 6 nonfiction books, encouraged me by all means to start from short stories as my #1 priority (not #6, as I planned to do it before).

Harish Singhal, who, after reading about my life, became buoyant and excited because my life has been a real thriller. He impel to write about it. Enthusiastically, he gave me confidence that my books would become successful.

ILLUSTRATION CREDITS

△ △ △

Front cover illustrations:
- a) Camels with pyramids meen_na/Dollar Photo Club
- b) On Mars Sergey Drozdov/Dollar Photo Club

Copyright page, back cover and spine: Sun symbol SCA-Graphics/Dollar Photo Club

Short Story #1
- a) WavebreakMediaMicro/Dollar Photo Club
- b) Javarman/Shutterstock

Short Story #2
Sergey Nivens/Dollar Photo Club

Short Story #3
Qoncept/Dollar Photo Club

Short Story #4
Romolo Tavani/Dollar Photo Club

Short Story #5
Sergey Nivens/Shutterstock

Short Story #6
Nuryudijes/Dollar Photo Club

Short Story #7
Andresr/Shutterstock

Short Story #8
O'SHI/Shutterstock

Illustration Credits

Short Story #9
    a) Everett historical/Shutterstock
    b) Air/Dollar Photo Club

Short Story #10
    Vadimmmus/Dollar Photo Club

Short Story #11
    Axellwolf/Dollar Photo Club

Short Story #12
    Monticello/Shutterstock

Short Story #13
    a) Indigolotos/Dollar Photo Club
    b) Vinicius Tupinamba/Dollar Photo Club

Short Story #14
    Syda Productions/Shutterstock

Short Story #15
    Pixelrobot/Dollar Photo Club

Short Story #16
    MasterLu/Dollar Photo Club

Short Story #17
    Littleny/Dollar Photo Club

Short Story #18
    Stockernumber2/Shutterstock

Short Story #19
    DevonSun/Shutterstock

Short Story #20
    Gustavo Frazao/Shutterstock

Illustration Credits

Short Stories #1–20
    Owl sits on a book/damato/Dollar Photo Club

Short stories #1 --#20
    The Moral of the Story, Notepad papers stacked, toldatezcan

"The Forces of Innovations...Conflict?,"
    an article by Carissa Giblin, *The Florida Engineering Journal*

THE AUTHOR'S, ALLA P. GAKUBA, BSCE, MAS, PhD, CONTRIBUTIONS TO ENGINEERING, TO NATIONAL WEALTH, AND TO WOMEN:

The Forces of Innovation...Conflict?
BY CARISSA GIBLIN, ARTICLE PROVIDED BY THE SOCIETY OF WOMEN ENGINEERS.
FLORIDA ENGINEERING JOURNAL, JANUARY 2004.

Many people ask Alla Gakuba how she innovates. She responds that she does not remember inventing something under normal circumstances; that is, without huge external and internal pressures. And it seems to be true. She came across a study while writing her dissertation for her PhD at George Washington University. The study surveyed thousands. of inventors asking them what factors were responsible for their innovations. The conclusion was great stress and pressure.

When Alla came to Baltimore, Maryland, in the beginning of the 1970s from the then USSR, she faced several environmental factors that created this pressure. There were few women engineers at the time. English was a new language to her. She knew only the metric system. Her husband was a physician working long hours, and they had two small children. It was the peak of the Cold War, and American engineers were paying close attention to Russian science and technology.

To her surprise, she was soon hired as a structural engineer. Never mind that Alla was not yet an engineer and that her English was only 4 months old. She had familiarized herself with the state building codes for a few days when the Chief Engineer told her her first project

Article by Carissa Giblin

would be designing a three span bridge over a ramp—completely on her own.

He handed her a field drawing depicting the location of the ramp. As she took the drawing, dizziness overwhelmed her. "How in the world am I going to design it?" ran through her head. In her memory she went back to engineering school in expectation to retrieve some information about the design. She could recall none. In school she took math, physics, chemistry, static, kinematics, dynamics, strength of material, and reinforced concrete and steel. There was no trace of bridge design. She walked back to her office in despair.

On her way home that evening she stopped at the bridge site and examined the parapets, decks, piers, columns, and footings of the nearby ramps. The next day she had a lot of ideas on how to design the bridge. Looking at the field drawing of the ramp, she recognized that she needed to know the soil pressure under the bridge. Randomly, she sketched a dozen of soil borings.

When she gave her sketch to the soil department and asked for pressure measurements, they took her seriously and asked when she needed the information. She realized then she was on the right track. She started focusing on the bridge design. Alla decided to stay, and the pressure was on.

Alla was able to draw upon her engineering problem-solving skills and determination to succeed. She divided the bridge into separate structures. Using common sense and applying math, physics, and strength of materials, she designed each component one by one. All the pieces fit together as a puzzle, and it became the bridge. The company assembled a team of engineers to check her design and they were astounded at the calculations she used. She told them that no one gave her guidance so she invented each of the calculations.

Her design was accepted 100%. As they learned how simple it was, her calculation methods became standard in the company. Alla had created her own way of designing instead of copying the standard processes. Some time later, Alla learned bridge design traditionally involved a team of engineers each specializing in a particular structure. The company had given her the whole bridge to design to gain insight on Russian engineering and also to limit her success as the only female engineer in the company. In the end the company was so impressed, they started searching for another woman engineer.

Alla's next contribution involved an I-95, ten span bridge with four ramps over the Patapsco River in downtown Baltimore. She was given an opportunity to design this bridge alone. This time, the company trusted and believed in her; otherwise they would not have put all their eggs into one basket. And she lived up to their expectations. Not only did she design the bridge and ramps, but she also introduced a new foundation design. It required 30% less construction materials than standard foundations. The revolutionary aspect was that Alla's foundation designs took just one page of calculations for each pier.

Usually the design of foundation for each pier required computer programs followed by 70–80 pages of hand calculations. Her calculations and drawings were wrapped up and sent to an outside consulting company to check if they were correct.

Several months later, the consultants' hundreds of pages of computer printouts and calculations produced the same result as the innovations that Alla had calculated on one page.

Article by Carissa Giblin

Later, Alla was given a challenge to find a solution to a spiral design for 5.5 miles of aerial structure for the Baltimore Subway.

Only later did she learn that before approaching her, the company advertised in professional magazines across the country for engineers who could design a spiral for the subway. The company received no response. This was because no one had designed this before and no one wanted to risk their career.

So, Alla took on the project. She started with a blank piece of paper. The chief engineer told her about two French books about the new Paris subway sections housed in the Library of Congress in Washington, DC. She retrieved the books along with a French-English Civil Engineering dictionary. (She knew some French, but not civil engineering French.) The information only reinforced that what is applicable in Paris was not applicable in Baltimore. Also, the books were not about calculations and design of a spiral. Instead, they were about the philosophy, problems, and approach to design.

In the end, she made her own invention and found the solution for a spiral design. She calculated one span by long hand. Then, it was very simple to mirror her calculations and run the remaining 550 or so spans through the computer. The company wrote that Alla found the solution for spiral design of the aerial structure and that they considered it to be the most difficult engineering design. As for Alla, the spiral design was a nightmare that she cannot forget easily.

Alla cannot attribute the above contributions to herself only. She was a product of time, place, and circumstances. The time was the 1970s, which were the best technological years in her generation. The place was the US where equal employment opportunity laws were taking shape. She was a Russian in the US during the Cold War, where the great technological and political competitions for the dominance of the world were taking place between the two countries. She was given opportunity and responsibility and she lived up to their expectations. If Alla had stayed in the USSR, she doubts that she would have produced such contributions. In her opinion, there is no incentive to innovate in a familiar supportive environment. There must be a pressure.

Next, Alla managed the construction of the Baltimore Subway.

Her next objective was to enlarge her knowledge and became a better person. She received her Master's Degree from John Hopkins University where professors and students encouraged her to earn a PhD so she could become a role model for other women. She did. She received her Doctoral degree from George Washington University with a major in Management of Science, Technology, and Innovations. She was the first woman to graduate in this field. Her dissertation was ranked among the top 5% of the 250–300 dissertations which have been written in the last 15 years.

Alla Gakuba, PhD is a business analyst and consultant in Tampa, Florida. She earned her Bachelor of Science in Civil Engineering from Odessa Civil Engineering University in the former Soviet Union.

(Reprint of this article was granted by *The Florida Engineering Journal* on January 19, 2015.)

HAVE YOU READ? BOOKS BY
ALLA P. GAKUBA, BSCE, MAS, PhD

Available wherever books sold

www.ingramcontent.com/pod-product-compliance
Lightning Source LLC
Chambersburg PA
CBHW021140080526
44588CB00008B/144